Beautiful Tragedies

A Dark Poetry Anthology

Compiled & Edited by Xtina Marie

A HellBound Books Publishing LLC Book
Houston TX

HellBound Books

A HellBound Books LLC Publication

Copyright © 2017 by HellBound Books Publishing LLC
All Rights Reserved

Cover and art design by HellBound Books Publishing LLC

**No part of this book may be reproduced, stored in a retrieval system, or transmitted by any means, electronic, mechanical, photocopying, recording or otherwise without written permission from the author
This book is a work of fiction. Names, characters, places and incidents are entirely fictitious or are used fictitiously and any resemblance to actual persons, living or dead, events or locales is purely coincidental.**

www.hellboundbookspublishing.com

Printed in the United States of America

Beautiful

Tragedies

HellBound Books

Foreword

Poetry means the world to me. It is through poetry that I express my deepest feelings. It is through poetry that I was first published. I had the best time compiling and editing this anthology.

Beautiful Tragedies is a collection of the most disturbing, haunting, tragic and beautiful poetry I've ever encountered. Love isn't always rainbows and unicorns. It's gut wrenching, it's consuming. It's beautifully tragic.

I am so very grateful to James Longmore of HellBound Books for allowing me complete editorial freedom to create this book of poetry collected from some incredibly talented writers. I know I speak for all the participating poets in the book when I say: Bless you for being a publisher with a soul.

To all the poets who contributed to this collection: Thank you so much, and I felt your pain, your horror, your sorrow, your longing.

Thank you, Debra B and Denise J. for helping me to spot imperfections when I thought my eyes were bleeding.

X

HellBound Books

Beautiful Tragedies - A Dark Poetry Anthology

Contents

Foreword	5
Alistair Cross	13
Words	
Footsteps	
Spark	
Duana Monroe	17
Dark Dalliance	
Ruswa Fatehpuri	18
The Madness of St George	
Inversely Square	
The Chemist Addresses His Patient Life Partner	
Jason Morton	24
Afraid	
Michael Picco	27
Charnel Love (To: E.A.P.)	
Shelby R. Thomas	28
Unrequited	
Nick Manzolillo	29
The Scab that Oozes	
Rebecca Kolodziej	31
Delirium	
Quinn Hernandez	33
Domestic Dispute	
Wish	
Backwash	
B. Bennett	39
Monster	
The River Glass	
A. Gonzales	45
Howling Winds	
Kimmy Alan	47
Queen Necrophilia	
Hell's Cannibals	
Muroidea Paranoia	
Dusty Davis	51
My Last Good-Bye	
The Conclusion	
The Days Have Passed	

HellBound Books

No More Tears to Cry
Georgia Williams   55
Him
Pain
Sadie Whitecoat   57
Emptie
Like a Raisin in the Sun
Morbid
Streya Colchester   61
Free
Hopeful Deductions
The Possessed
L.M. Sabourin   67
One Night at Broadway Video
Serena Daniels   70
Tethered
Drown
James Michael Shoberg   72
Restless legs
Masquerade
Attention, Please
Benjamin Blake   80
An American Tragedy
Chloroform
Errant Heart
Pamela Morris   83
Con Fuoco
Fierce Warrior of the Left-Hand Path
Brandon Ryals   90
The Kiss
Love's Damnation
Sorrow's Kiss
Heartache
My Depression
David Whippman   94
Hard History Lesson
Hollywood Divorce
Frank Coffman   96
Residual Murder

Beautiful Tragedies - A Dark Poetry Anthology

Phil Wolters   103
Ruminations of Death while Stopped at a Traffic Light in Calgary
Charles Gramlich   105
One Recipe for Disaster
Stained
Crown of Flies
Denise Jury   108
Scarred Heart
Haiku 1
Haiku 2
Haiku 3
Haiku 4
Ryan Woods   113
Bleed, Bitch, Bleed
Humble Pie
Slipknots and Razorblades
The Start of the End is only Half the Story
Love's Last Breath
Richard Alan Long   128
A Martyr for the Brokenhearted
I've Got My Summer Right Now
The Woman at the Window
James H. Longmore   130
No One Dies Instantly
Brandy Delight   134
The Final Filter
Wedding Vows
Ancient Friend
Forrest J Hiler   137
Six
Pull the Trigger
Twisted Mentality
Hades Rising   144
Underneath the Mourning Star
Crimson Lips of Death
Splinter in the Heart
Rana Kelly   152

Boy
Carrion
Wolves
Jason Prenatt   157
King of Worms
In Utero Cover Art
Venus in Furs
Paul Bridgeman   161
When I See You Again
Burn!
Melysza Jackson   166
I Stand Alone
Broken
19 and Foolish
Razors Edge
R A Bane   172
Opium Dreams
Farewell
Elaine Bezuidenhout   175
Blood Red Rose
Eleventh Hour
The Soul That Could Not Find Love
James D. Merwin   178
The Ferryman's Journey
I Wonder
When Will It
Paul B. Morris   183
Hey, Maggie
The Grey Man
Lemmy Rushmore   187
Vestiges
This Hell That I'm In
Remnants
Becky Narron   192
Without You
Linz Bassett   194
Shattered Trust
New Beginnings

Beautiful Tragedies - A Dark Poetry Anthology

I Am Empty
Let the Past Go
The Dark Side of Love
Gerri R. Gray — 199
Today I Feel
Dark Craving
Memento Mori (Christmas Eve)
Richard Archer — 203
Cursed
Book Lover
Mathias Jansson — 207
Confessions of Adrian Black - ghosts that I have fucked:
Countess Marybeth
Lady Morgana
The Borgia's twin
Madame Marie
Schoolmistress Susan
Glen Damien Campbell — 212
Virginia
John T. M. Herres — 213
Silent Screams
Gocni Schindler — 214
Bi-Polar Super Bitch
Leah Negron — 218
Inner Demons
Too Tight
Death's Poet
Craig Detheridge — 221
Chocolate Box Love
The Old Fallow Field - *A Rhyming Horror Story*
Shanta Nicole — 226
Be Still, My Love
Xtina Marie — 227
He Doesn't Know
Love Isn't Enough (A Microshort)
Love Kills
A Most Horrible Pain
Her Love Has No End

HellBound Books

Alistair Cross
Words

In the history of language
How was it decided
Which words to string together
And in whom they'd be confided?

How did we decide
Which words to leave unspoken?
And when did we decide
To describe our hearts as broken?

Who said when all was said?
Who said when all was done?
And to whom can we give thanks
For the pleasure of the pun?

Synonyms and homonyms
Who dreamed up these things?
Who gave so much substance
To such nonsensical utterings?

Who turned these words to stanza
Dispersing rhapsody and verse?
What brought on vulgarity
And who was the first to curse?

I ask these questions frequently
But I know the answer to just one
And I'm sure that you'll agree with me
If you've ever had this done

If you've ever said, "I love you,"

And only silence greets your plea
Then you know, my friend, that silence
Was the first obscenity

Footsteps

I know you heard me on the stairs
I know you heard me call
I know you heard me say 'goodnight'
But you never looked up, at all

And I know you heard the closing door
And my footsteps down the hall
But you didn't say a word to me
And that somehow said it all

Spark

So now you see the spark
I harbored in the darkness
And you can tell the world
I'm hell-bound and I'm heartless

Did you think that I'd be nothing
But hurt, hollow and haunted
When you turned us into all the things
You knew I never wanted

When you began to play
These complicated games
These tangled up entanglements
That stain love's sacred name

You're determined to be angry
For one reason or another
You're happy when you hate me
So rage on, my wayward lover

I can offer you no freedom
I can't save you from yourself
For your mind is your own prison
And your heart is your own hell

But what would I have given
For one last time-lapsed touch
Anything, my darling…
I wanted you that much

Duana Monroe
Dark Dalliance

If I could, I'd make a memory jar of you. I'd poke holes in the lid and keep you, take you out, touch your boyish face, lick your fleshy lips, and press you to me. But, I'm frightened I wouldn't stop.

I want your wit, but how can I fondle it? I'd suck your brilliance and squeeze your humor. I wouldn't stop... how could I? I would ride your darkness like a pagan goddess screwing the sky. I'd swallow you whole. Your words are like candy so I might press your voice box between my tits, fucking it until your breath went away.

You'd give it. I know. You'd let me gobble your thoughts and rub your soul to tormented completion.

I'll send you a can opener and a formaldehyde filled jar with a self-addressed stamped envelope.

With a promise.

I'll hide what you send inside me. When I'm touching myself, I'll be touching you.

I'm the ghoul for you.

Ruswa Fatehpuri
The Madness of St George

The dragon's snout is silver steel
Needle bright and prickness
In light that lives and bends
Reflected off curved objects
Dirt beneath my skin and naked
But for the filthy remnant rag of faith
My mother would not use to wipe the windows.
Tattered whores - all that I could afford -
Have marvelled at my scars
Emptied out my corpse fat purse
Of looted rings and ornaments

The dragon has a belly full of fire
Sweet excoriance
Embouchure and kiss. Petit Mort
Life. Or moments masquerading at a life
I could.
God damn you all. I could forswear her call
Embrace not death, nor vanquishing
But sieving out each breath behind
The constant siren call, the vapour wraith

The dragon's tail, foursquare and death.
I draw it as a sword and cast it out
Weeping as accelerants
Seep, soak and evanesce

Say it. Sing it. Go out, rejoice
For George has slain the dragon
Today. Only today

Inversely Square

The time before the comet came
Was ordered. Change that could be measured
Mapped out and predicted
A perfect waltz, the perfect partner

With mighty telescopes, we parsed the stars
To see ourselves reflected in their stately symmetry
Celestially safe in the heartbeat of the heavens

We saw the comet from afar
We plotted out its course
A marvel that would pass us by
An asymptotic air kiss and goodbye

Mathematics is weak
It measures hearts in inches and the height of mercury
Certain in its casino
    of probabilities
Imagining new laws
    for lawless strange attraction
Ignorant of the calculus of chance

The moon ripped in a million pieces
Falling like confetti at a second wedding
Our dance descended into chaos
Transcended in the frenzy
To knowing there was more than order.
Finding fractures in our careful arcs
Our diablos and conic sections
Devils hidden in the details
Deep beneath the curves

So brief. This one event
In our 'til death time horizon
The comet that changed everything
And wandered out into the void
More debris in its tail

Amidst the gases swirling
Circling with the chunks of rock and ice
Planetary flotsam, some remnants of our moon
My inch-cubed, unbeating flesh
Frozen and pressureless

The Chemist Addresses His Patient Life Partner

Your long wait is done my dear
Your patience is rewarded
I have found the secret of your love
The formula is perfected

For decades I have pounded
The pestle of my alchemy
In this quicksilver distillate
Is your liquid love for me?

I have unlocked the secret
Of how your passion flares and burns
And with a single drop of blood
I give your just returns

Your arm, my dear a single vein
Or a cut upon your thumb
A bitten lip is all I need
And the potion will be done

Awake my sweet, for now I can
Love you as you love me
From the prison of my lame compassion
You can at last be free

Your arm, my dear, is all I ask
This half-life will be ended
But why so still and cold my dear?
How have I offended?

I am singed and cut and blinded
To make my heart beat as your heart
I have poured our years together
Into this fragile art

Have the decades of your waiting
Made love unravel and unfold?
What is this pallor of your skin?
Why are your hands so cold?

Awake my love, end your wait
For my hard heart's energy
Rise my dear, give me your hand
Shake off this lethargy

Jason Morton
Afraid

I am I – lost like a child,
Wide eyed and staring brought to my knees,
I don't feel that this is reality,
This is love?
It feels so strange and broken.

I am I – Watching the world pass,
Like time fading into empty thought,
The wind wails like a banshee,
All courage fades,
And I push you away again.

I am I – and I am going to lose you?
Are you going to run away when you see me for what I am?
A distance will come between us,
We will never be close again.
As I break what is fragile.

I am I – a monster that ruins everything good,
A child who is afraid,
Everything starts to come together
I begin to break it apart,
Will I ever tear down these walls?

I am I – I am afraid you won't like me,
I am afraid you won't love me,
Who can love me,
When I don't love me?

So I begin to push you away into the darkness of my rotting day.

I am I – cold and vile
The fear is real, but I am just a big child,
How can you stay,
When the eleventh hour draws near.
And I push you to the brink with the cuts on my arms?

I am I – afraid to love,
I am afraid to try,
I am afraid of life,
I am afraid of dying,
I am so fucked up I don't care anymore!

I am I – lost and broken,
Taking it out on you,
Though you have wised up,
You have run away,
Now you are as broken as me.

I am I - adding to the scars,
Bloody razor in my hand,
I pushed you away,
You tried but were broken,
And now I am alone again.

I am I – fucked up and broken,
Tragically misunderstood,
I was so afraid,
That I would be me again,
That I repeatedly did it over and over and over again.

Am I insane?

Am I afraid?
Am I unloved?
Am I just fucked up?
Am I lost?
Am I just afraid?

Michael Picco
Charnel Love (To: E.A.P.)

No soul resides in my lover's eyes —
no passion, warmth, or gleam.
My lover's sighs are bellows-borne
and commingle with my screams.
Neither doleful dirge, nor wailing keen
will mar my Love's lost dreams…
for my Love is cold…dead…and old…
as loathsome as the lust it weans.

Shelby R. Thomas
Unrequited

She screamed at herself in her head
Forever believing she could be
Anywhere near what he desired.
She had not been blessed with great beauty,
Nor a body like those all men seek to find.
She was plain;
No different than any common woman
In any city or town.
The gifts she possessed
Were also the curses that plagued her.
An innocent heart beat within her chest,
And it drew the attention of many who barely had a heart of their own.
She was trusting,
To a fault;
They knew she simply needed to hear that they cared for her,
And she was putty in their hands.
She desired one simple thing:
To be loved.
Upon hearing a few pretty little words,
She offered her heart freely,
Expecting only love in return.

Nick Manzolillo
The Scab that Oozes

There was a man who drowned.

A year later I saw him
again
at my wedding, standing by the cake
flesh washed pale in a suit of seaweed
clutching a ship in a bottle.

He was told to leave and promptly collapsed
into a hastily mopped spillage of sails, shards, and
high tide bile.

A big day and an uproarious night
followed by a morning with my head in the toilet.
A damp footprint trail back to bed
the drowned man lingers behind her
whispering a tongue of clicking, starving, jittery
crabs
first mistaken for soft waves kissing upon sand

High tide overrides Febreze

The drowned man aches, drying out
he watches our pyrrhic sleep with clammy sweat
rimmed frog eyes
slouching among the ancient wine stains of the
armchair.

I never did learn to swim.

A puddle above drips
missing my outstretched tongue
dribbling along her cheek
I rollover
and lap it away
and I need

I will flick that photo by her bed
and place it down
down by its own weight

I will slither in behind her,
outline her smooth, parting arms and her powerful kick
I will plug the holes in her nostrils and kiss the back of her lungs

The drowned man runs a tidal hand through his hair of eelgrass
belching a point Nemo croak, his gills appearing like slits along his windpipe

He can adapt,
at the bottom of any sea
But first,
he must search for company

Rebecca Kolodziej
Delirium

What do you know of pain? The suffering of my mind.
A fractured memory alive with traumas of the past,
Each night they refuse to let me sleep,
Within my nightmares I swim too deep,
Unable to escape, unable to surface,

My bed, the open ocean,
The blankets, the cold sea,
And though I feel myself sinking,
Somehow it comforts me,

I feel as if I am floating,
Somewhere I'm at peace,
Yet there is no peace amongst my dreams
Only lucid, vicious beasts

My eyes slowly open,
And what I see haunts my mind
Black figures loom above me,
Faceless masses with insidious smiles

"we know that you are dying, we feed off the pain you supply?"
They whisper to me in dead voices as empty tears escape my eyes
"why must you torment me so? Why can't you just let me live in peace?"
A mocking laugh surrounds my watery tomb,
"but soon you shall be deceased."

I had my time they told me, and I abused my gift at life,
My pain has been my punishment, my release the edge of a knife.
"but why? I continued asking, though I knew my words would fail,
"death cares not for sympathy, your suffering grows stale.
The time for you has come to finally free yourself from pain,
We are here to guide you, to convince you that you're to blame."

With every word they uttered I knew that they were right,
The suffering of my existence was because I failed at life.
Black hands swirl above me, like smoke hovers over water,
I stare my demons in the eye as they choke me into torture.

I will never be free, even if death I will remain in pain,
What do you know of my pain? The suffering of my mind…

Quinn Hernandez
Domestic Dispute

she was in our bedroom
pretending to be cleaning
but she was just avoiding me
I asked her something
and was met with her silence
the silent treatment
her punishment for my complaints
it always amazed me
how quickly a day could go south
cause I failed to learn from my past
but was it all my fault?
didn't we both fall into
the same old traps?
our arguments are a recording
dialogue of déjà vu,
always the money
and her lack of discipline
her lack of caring
for what I am going through
I am too controlling
I can't control my anger
I treat her like a child
and I say,
"it's because you act like a child."
I'm not hearing her
and she's not hearing me
the same sick cycle
we had both endured
for over twenty years

doesn't something have to give?
I call out again
and again, no response
she knows me too well
as I know her
and I fall into that trap
my temperature rises
my goat fully gotten
I'm done asking
now I march down the hall
raising my voice

my words echo off
the silent walls of our home
the one we built together
the one I will surely lose
and now I reach the doorway
to our bedroom
where we held each other
and made love
and I see her mimicking
the actions of folding laundry
at her feet is her body
soaked in an impossible amount
of blood
and next to her
my white body lies
my gaping wound
the only color I have left
the scene brings it all back
the stale old argument
the childish hate from before
and then the realization
we'll never go back
to the way things were
the lost word, "we"

is now dead like us
forever
something within
dies for me to cry
but I can't
that is a luxury reserved
for the living
and even if I could
that trick will no longer work
there is no amount of tears
that can wash this away
but still
I try to say I am sorry
and tell her that I still love her
but it just comes out
as anger, as blame

and of course, those words
are met with silence
defeated, I turn and go back
to the solitary confinement
of my corner
our living room
it has become painfully obvious
that she is done talking to me
for a very long time

Wish

He has in the past fantasized about being the star at his family's funeral, where everyone he knew lined up to give him their heartfelt condolences.

And though he could never understand why, he knew he needed this: the attention his expendable family would garner him. This precious gem was something he had missed his whole life.

Now he thinks of his family on the road headed toward Chicago to see his wife's sister, and how work had kept him home. He thought of loosened lug nuts and prayed for his dream call.

He sat back and practiced crying.

Backwash

she was a friend for a day
now you wish she'd go away
she fulfilled your need
by ejecting your seed
it went the same as the others
those dime-a-dozen lovers
a notch for another
soon to be mother
no more of the same song
of what happened was wrong
because you don't care for
what was shared before
the problems she'd shown
are hers all alone
you don't have the time
for that old familiar whine
the girls that you played
shared fates self-made
too good to be true
usually means harm for you
she failed to learn that rule
now she plays the fool
she could have said no
now she pays for your show
she will try and blame Cupid
rather than admit she was stupid
and now thanks to your plan
she'll never again trust a man

but a smile returns once more
to the face you called whore
as now your smile fades
as she confesses she has AIDS

B. Bennett

Monster

If you were a monster, I could save you,

even if it meant that I'd be left black and blue and other hues that I refuse

to name.

I saw myself in the brown of your eyes - such lies disguised as lullabies - yet, it's all the same.

If you were a vicious beast I would feed off of your darkness and insecurities - I would be the best me to stop the seed

from growing any further.

Because that's what girls like me do - they never give up and refuse

to allow the beast's spirit to be trampled, or his will tested - even though the love he offers is merely a sample

of what he could give if he didn't make things so difficult.

If you were a wolf, and me, a lamb - I would allow you to dissect everything that I am.

I would let you find the underlying madness in my blue eyes –

I would let you feed off of me until everything left is a facade –

I would let you cut me deep, even if it meant losing everything –

because I need a monster, you see

to feed the darkness growing in me.

The River Glass

Black swirls and white faces

staring
and
swearing

in return.

Don't you

hate
the
rage

when it is caged in?
Didn't you forget

your
frail
ways?

You said when you were through

it
would
all
come
back
to
you.

When all was forgotten, you were locked in

in the world of sin
which we call our home
all alone.

You swore you would come back for her, but never
did

and
when
she
would
drown

you were no longer her keeper.

Everything was cold, for you drew deep her sorrow.
A "man" you became

helpless
and
fragile.

You couldn't, and you never would
save her.
Cold motionless lips
would no longer kiss your chest.

The pain you created, you brought her to
Hell.

As the grim reaper

draws
up
his

arms

only to cast a curse.
Satan himself didn't have the nerve.
She fell because you dropped her.

Roses
would
fall
from
the
sky

a love once strong would turn to hate.

That was her fate,
to mourn.

For you were the one, the only, who could stop her pain.

Although time after time, you would
forget her.

Turn to the river to forget your scorn, turn away the demons

the
face
of
bliss.

Nothingness.

You failed the present.

To face your flaws,
in a world like this,
the only place to go
is the River Glass.

A. Gonzales
Howling Winds

Sitting silently underneath the burning oak,
I realize that deep inside of me, there is an unknown demon etched into my soul

A soul containing demonic visions - cursed with powers not of this world - demons whisper twisted words in my mind

Branches crackle and bow down from the stress of the flames which consume them

My face feels every degree change – my body heating up as the flames draw closer and closer.

I stand and open my black eyes, much like the depths of my soul, I spread my wings and grab my staff which was forged by the hands of who's name we shall not speak.

Staring off into the distance down the burning hillside, I see chaos - destruction lies among the waste in my path of evil.
Standing behind me are the demons that follow my every command. I send a wave down to scour the area
And as I do so, I see a hideous beast coming straight for me

It's eyes are red like the flames that are swirling above me, dogs of doom snarl and walk with it as it inches closer and closer.

At that moment, I burst into the sky and look down at the beast as I get closer to strike him, I stop in mid-flight only to realize...

I was Staring at myself all along.

Someone I didn't recognize, but clearly it was my demons playing games with my mind.

Kimmy Alan
Queen Necrophilia

He loved her so much
He loved her too much
He could not give her up
So, after her last breath
He had her stuffed
Posed her ready for love
But taxidermy was not enough
To keep his lover from decomp
And she began to rot
The air became fragrant
With a scent beyond repugnant
Making neighbors distraught
Finally, the police came to knock
What they discovered was a shock
Reprobate they asked, "WTF?"
"How could you do something so corrupt?"
His answer;
"Once you get use to the smell
You'll find
She's actually quite a wonderful gal!"

Hell's Cannibals

Blood and flesh, flesh and blood
Time to feed the devil
And watch him fuck
Virgin pleading, see her bleeding
Satan's grinning, his stomach's churning
She is so tender and succulent
The master has feasted, and is sated
For a taste, we've patiently waited
May we have bite, or a bone to suck?
A virgin meal, sweet as veal
Uncorrupted flesh, par broil till ideal
Evil cannot eat enough, of flesh untouched
We are encouraging, girls who are listening
Preserve your purity, for the more worthy
Hell values virginity, more than the Holy Trinity
So, keep that hymen intact
On all Hallowed Eve
We'll be back, for a snack!

Muroidea Paranoia
Inspired by Kafka's 'Metamorphosis'

Like Lucifer's fall from grace
I dropped from the human race
Neurotic paranoid schizoaffective with addiction
Into the dark I retreated with my mental affliction
Dilapidating in desperation I prowl and sneak
Nearsightedly on hands and knees I rummage slink and creep
Scavenging the sewers, gutters, dumpsters, clutter and alleys
Of garbage and sewage for digestible grubbery
Filthy frizzled frazzled mangy hair crawling with lice and fleas
My surviving mustard-colored teeth decay with disease
Like tusks over my withered lips only a few remain
My dirty untrimmed fingernails are yellow and frayed
I'm harmless, yet people are startled at my sight
So I prowl in the lonely shadows of the night
My humanity is slowly disintegrating
Tweaking ticking twitching scratching shivering
Body constantly moving in psychomotor agitation
Chemical mortification of the flesh in declination
Some dumpsters are better than others
Some swill and garbage has more to offer
My inflamed olfactory detects odorants of molding
Leading me to a steel cornucopia of bakery leavings

Where I feast on musty maggot-infested sweet breads
With such abandon I'm oblivious to the iron jaws of death
"Hey Jack…Jack!
Come here quick!
Look at the huge rat
I caught in my trap!"

NOTE FROM THE AUTHOR: Diagnosed with cancer can be a humbling experience. Though I never had a substance abuse problem, the synthetic opiates I took, along with the effects of chemo, were devastating to my psyche. Plagued with insomnia, I'd wander the streets at night. I looked like a wreck. My hair fell out in patches. Due to acute dry mouth, my teeth literally rotted out. People avoided me like the plague. I never felt so alone. For the first time in my life, I identified with society's outcasts. One night, I had a horrible nightmare that I was trapped in a dumpster crawling with rats. I awoke drenched in sweat and trembling in fear. My poem is a dramatic reflection of those very dark days.

Dusty Davis
My Last Good-Bye

I'm lying here with nothing left to give.
Trying to figure out a reason for me to even live.
But through everything I've been through, I'm still alive.
Well I'm tired of fighting to just survive.
I've been living on hopes and dreams,
And crying through the night with no one to hear my screams.
I can't keep going through this life wondering why.
So I'm giving up and saying my last good-bye.

The Conclusion

All I wanted for so many years
In minutes disappears.
The darkest colors are looking clear.
The end will soon be here.
You tell me that you never lied,
But you always cried.
Unending suicide, look into my eyes,
And you will see where my soul lies.
I beg for forgiveness on my knees,
Crying in the night, hoping that no one sees.
I wait out in the rain, with my soul full of pain.
I stand alone but it never shows.
For no one cares if I'm here or there, whether I'm alive or dead
Lying face down on my bed.
For life is just an illusion
And death is the conclusion.

The Days Have Passed

Too many days have passed me by.
I have nothing left except the tears I cry.
Now I'm alone and don't know why.
Nobody is here to tell good-bye.
I don't know what I'm going to do.
Sick of this life I'm going through.
Too many days have passed me by.
I'm all alone except for the tears I cry.

No More Tears to Cry

I pray to God to help me, but He just turns away.
I'm begging Him for Death, so He forces me
through another day.
I'm sorry, I tried to be strong and believe.
But living this way forever, I just can't conceive.
So take me now, just let me lay down and die.
I have nothing left to give to you, I have no more
tears to cry.

Georgia Williams
Him

Why did this happen to me?
Why can't I just be free?
Why shatter my heart?
It made me fall apart.
My dignity took away
To never see the light of day.
The light turned to dark
He leaves his mark.
For my thoughts are never stopping
My life forever moping.
I cannot forget my broken past
My happiness will not last.
The tears keep on falling
And the fear keeps on crawling.
Lurking in the darkness
He strikes…with a likeness.
I feel pain
Makes me go insane.
I'm now so lost
Took away what I needed most.
I've been marked…cursed
If only it was reserved.
My life will never be the same
I will never forget…when he came.

Pain

I feel pain
Glass inside my brain.
Inside I'm dying
Outside I'm crying.
Trying to hold on
Losing my grip but staying strong.
Slipping away into the shadows
I feel the pain. Shot by arrows.
It takes over me
But I am still free.
The pain's deadly grip
Taking me on a wild trip.
It can't hold on
Because I stay strong.
I fight it. I win.
Pain is such a sin
But the pain never goes.

Sadie Whitecoat
Emptie

The absence of beating *haunts* me
And all surrounding.
I'm curious enough
I may crack, or cut open my chest cavity.
No love inside, I've lost the capacity.
Searching for self by self-mutilation
And just when I'm thinking I need not dig deeper-
My chest chamber swings wide OPEN!

I'm confused...
To see hollowness, I see vacant-ness
Void space, It's just emptiness...

I no longer reside inside but maintain outsides
Of this gloomy disguise, the soul blind has
Given the rank of goddess.

The screaming underneath my bosom is endless.
I default back to nameless I wish I did not exist.
Whose idea, was it?
To put on this planet a troubled soul for which no match existed
God, are you sick?

Is this for your entertainment?
I believe I've found my mirror and I'm tricked by skewed reflections
And I sink gracefully into, the deepest depression

That will endlessly worsen.

I know I was put on this earth just to see
How long until an angel's heart ceases to beat.
My lonely life spent searching for love and it doomed me
There is no light at the end,
Only darkness and defeat.

Like a Raisin in the Sun

I send neurotoxins direct to my brain
My only hope is to deaden the pain
And to put an end to thoughts that race
Over memories of you and your sweet embrace.
Brain damage hopeful, mind erase.

Dreams of you torment me to this day
Sleepless nights with unwelcoming hags
all dedicated to my wasting away
Rotten cells, decayed smells
You ate me alive and now it eats at my brain!
Full of holes now but still just the same as the ones in my heart.
Seeping begins and I struggle and strain
To control bleeding that comes down like rain...
And I won't rest my thoughts
Until blood begins to clot.

Morbid

Pinpoint pupils are not permitted.
Poking holes in yourself until leaks have sprung,
And the blood spill is endless.
My favorite way to see
My favorite shade of red...

Constant with crying and self-mutilation
For only the sake of my own humiliation
People can be so cruel...

Time seeps out of me just a blood from
An unburdened uterus when the moon says its time.
I wonder when time will call out to me...

I always believed you didn't exist,
and that I shouldn't...

Streya Colchester
Free

I'm gripping the door handle with all my might
Trying to keep it from turning
You're on the other side trying to pick the lock
If you get in I'm going to get hurt
My heart is pounding
Have you given up
Are you taking a break
I grab my backpack
I fill it with essentials
I wish I could take more, but I can't risk it
I need to run
I open the door a sliver
Listening
Nothing still
Maybe this time I'll get lucky
Maybe this time I'll get away
Now I'm poking my head out
Tensed up
Ready to shut the door and lock it again
I don't see movement
I don't hear anything
Quietly as I grab my bag and head for the door
A fearful mixture of hurrying and trying to not be heard
I slide the chain off
I unlock the door
I'm so close now

Taking a deep breath, I open the door
Too loud
I hurry outside
My heart beating faster
I take off running
I have to put as much distance between us as quickly as possible
I don't know where I'll go
All I know is I'm never going back
I'm free

Hopeful Deductions

Suddenly awake
What was that
That noise
Hold my breath
Listening
There it is again

Look over
Not hubby
He's fast asleep
Then what was that

Was it a burglar
Was it the front door
Someone's footsteps

Footsteps
A murderer
No
Too horrible
Let's try something else
What else is there

Kids out of bed
Not likely
Big day
What then

Was it
Was it a spirit
Friendly spirit

Evil spirit
Vengeance
Havoc
Cruel joke

Listening again
Nothing

Still listening
Still nothing

Nothing
Whatever it was
It's stopped
It's done
I hope

The Possessed

It is inside me
This thing
This voice
This nightmare I fight

Every day
Every night

I fight it in my dreams

It sings sweetly
It cajoles
It coerces
It gets angry and rages

Though I fight
I do not always win

I cannot control myself when it wins
When it takes over, I am not myself

I scream
I rant
I rave
I threaten
I curse

Or sometimes

I cry
I despair
I disappear inside

Sometimes the loss is sudden
I know not what happened
Other times it is the slow turning of a tide
The same when I regain control

Though I am joyous
Giddy with delight
Inside of me is a battle
A beast
A never-ending fight

L.M. Sabourin
One Night at Broadway Video

She was working late that evening
At the local video store.
She had about an hour to go
'Til she could close and lock the door.

She was waiting on a lady
When the phone began to ring.
She answered, "Broadway Video,"
But the caller said not a thing.

She hung the phone up with a frown,
And continued with the sale,
But the customer would later say
That her face turned slightly pale.

About ten minutes had gone by
When, again, she heard the phone.
She had to run to answer it,
'Cause she was working all alone.

When she picked up the receiver,
A chill ran up her spine.
She heard somebody breathing,
But no voice came on the line.

About a half an hour went by,
And the ringing began again.

She had just begun a new account
For an extremely nice young man.

The gentleman would later say
That when she took the call,
She loudly said, "Stop calling me!"
And her tears began to fall.

The young man said that, as he left,
He saw her lock the door.
And he thought he heard her saying,
"I can't take this anymore!"

She turned on the alarm, and left,
Then got into her car.
She hit the gas and drove away,
But didn't get too far.

For then, she heard her cell phone ring,
From where it lay, inside her purse.
She knew, in that brief second,
Things had gone from bad to worse.

She never saw the stranger's face.
She only saw the flashing knife.
The killer came from her back seat,
And slashed away her precious life.

The sheriff, on the news that night,
Said the killer was quite neat,
And that not a shred of evidence

Could be found on either seat.

They found her boyfriend's body.
It was stuffed inside the trunk.
He was there, amid the beer cans,
Used rubbers, and other junk.

The TV said the murders
Were the strangest seen in years.
The papers said the killer
Had taken gory souvenirs.

She was my husband's final fling.
My hatred for them lingers.
I may have left them both behind,
But I took their heads and fingers.

Serena Daniels
Tethered

You tie me down
With those chains around my heart
I am a slave to you, my master
I am lost
I am alone but for you
As you have seen fit
You say that barbed wire connects our hearts and that is why I cannot be let go
Perhaps that is indeed true
For if I move, my heart will be torn to shreds and I will bleed out
However, you would suffer the same fate
Perhaps this is the only escape route for me
Yes, death will be preferable to this living torment
Of being your love captive

Drown

It's the only way out; you tell me
It's the only way that we can be together
I am not sure if this way is best
Surely there is a place so far away
Where no one knows our names, our faces
There is nowhere to run, nowhere to hide; you say
They will never understand our love
I am so scared
I should not be
But I am
What if it takes too long?
What if it is painful?
I don't have time to think
Because you have taken my hand and pulled us from the cliff top
We float until the waves take us

James Michael Shoberg
Restless Legs

Sure, Bobby's distress was irrational, for he feared scorpions stinging his toes—

And in Pennsylvania, there were no such crawlies, as anyone sensible knows.

Well, none to be seen roaming freely about, those arachnids, which haunted the child,

But lying in bed filled with unfounded angst, he cared not if they thrived in the wild.

Each night, he believed he could feel them exploring his legs to the soles of his feet,

And petrified, Bobby convinced himself he saw activity under the sheet.

He was, of course, right, as the movements he saw were quite real and not optical tricks;

However, the root wasn't scorpions—it was his dread-induced, impulsive kicks.

So, Bobby had tried to distract himself in the pursuit of some measure of sleep.

That's hard to achieve though, if what's being counted are nightmarish scorpion-sheep.

One evening, young Bobby, amidst an assault from the maddening, fictional pests,

Had screamed out, "ENOUGH!" Then he tore back the covers to challenge his unwanted guests.

But all he observed were his quivering feet, which, apart from the gooseflesh, were bare.

Exhausted, he growled at the phantasmal creeps, "If you want it so badly, then THERE!

The bed is all yours; fill the blankets with eggs! As for me, I'll be down on the couch!"

And that's when he placed his foot into the slipper containing a Black Widow. "OUCH!"

Masquerade

Our Devin never quite fit in among the other boys.

The lacy, fair, and delicate were all his secret joys.

He'd rather play the damsel than the hero any day—

Though hid what made him happy, as he dreaded what we'd say.

Despite the risk, he'd often steal into his sister's room

To try on pretty things, and there, in private, he would bloom.

How sad it was to watch our child, for, naturally, I knew—

But I could not relieve the pain, so day by day it grew.

I wondered, "Will he come to me? Will Devin share his ache?"

In time he did—reluctantly—I still can see him shake.

Uncertain—first, he faltered, "I'm not sure I can explain.

Mom, I don't feel this body was intended for my brain."

As we sat in the kitchen, my poor son began to cry.

Between each deep and tortured sob, he just repeated, "Why?"

My arm around his shoulders, I consoled him—well, I tried.

"It takes more than a mirror, Dev, to know ourselves inside.

And we will always love you—as you are—so don't forget."

I misread his inspired smile, and that's my worst regret.

If I believed that I had helped with just a kindly word,

That notion soon was disabused by piercing screams I heard.

Yes, foolishly, I thought that I had aided him in strife

And failed to notice Devin made off with my butcher's knife.

The bathroom door was partly closed. I only saw his back,

Which was my last sane memory before it all went black.

For as he turned, now lidless eyes spilled tears of brightest red.

Yet he was grinning all the while with no lips on his head.

His gory face hung from his jaw—the skin, an empty sheath.

"I hoped that when I peeled it off there'd be a girl beneath."

Attention, Please

Poor Dan was enslaved by the notice he craved and his hunger voraciously grew.

In spite of the praise that his antics would raise, he was glum with the sum that they drew.

So itchy was he, for awareness you see, he auditioned for all the school shows.

And once he was cast—which occurred at long last—he bragged, "Yes! I'M the one whom they chose!

When I tread 'the boards,' there'll be talk of awards, as I stupefy, startle, and stun.

Then both Mom and Dad will be proud that they had such a marvel as me for their son!"

But bleak was the fact that his characters lacked any qualities well-worth applause.

The raven-haired boy, with his quixotic ploy, always failed to evoke oohs and ahhs.

"They pay me no mind. Are they cruel or just blind? I need some small assent of my skill!"

In truth, though, his need was a bottomless greed no ovation could dare hope to fill.

Dan's heart wasn't bad. It was lonely and sad, and his bluster held panic at bay.

He deeply believed that the nods he received were
what kept him from fading away.

"A moment's regard, is that really too hard?" he'd
direct at a parent or friend.

The slew he had gained (most of which had been
feigned) did not stifle his dread of the end.

Obsessed with the fear that he'd soon disappear, Dan
sequestered himself in his room,

Vowing not to emerge till he'd conquered the
scourge he imagined would lead to his doom.

"Is it really me? Do I falter to be the sensational Dan
I surmise?

No, surely I'm due. Such a thing can't be true," and
with that, his self-doubt was revised.

Dan practiced the jokes he decided would coax the
attention required to thrive.

"Yes, humor, and bits, and hilarious skits are my
best bet for staying alive!

I dare them to flout, all the things I've worked out—
each new parody, sendup, and spoof."

But flout them they did, for annoyed with the kid,
those he tried to amuse grew aloof.

Forsaking the plan, which did nothing for Dan, he
withdrew from indifferent stares.

"What more can be done? I've been witty and fun.
Why, the fault isn't mine it is theirs!"

So, vacant of hope, and unable to cope, he obsessively studied his face

And swore, as expected, that what was reflected was what they all saw—empty space.

The torturous wait for his imminent fate had grown greater than young Dan could bear,

Defeated, he tread to the foot of his bed, where he sat and gave in to despair.

Accepting his death, he took one final breath as he watched his hand fade from his wrist.

Then all that Dan wore slipped away to the floor as he changed into transparent mist.

To give oneself grief with a foolish belief, is quite silly and also a shame;

But have faith enough in preposterous stuff, and you'll end up like…uh…what's his name?

Benjamin Blake
An American Tragedy

This isn't going to end well
The stabs and twists of fate
Will leave at least one of us bled out
Though, most likely both
The warning signs are more than evident
They're written in those late night falling stars
And read in stacks of tarot cards
One doesn't need to be psychic
To know
This isn't going to end well

Chloroform

Time turned on itself
And I'm all out of knives
Woke to another dreary dream
Of killers lurking in public parks
Searching for a riper victim

Inside-out eyes
Burrowing into my own
The urge has always been there
Ever since I was a young child
Bleeding from the side of the head
And collecting bones

Laying spent
In leaf-covered loam
Shivering uncontrollably
Stained with dirt and synovial fluid
As new ghosts dance in the ballroom
Of this wayward skull

Errant Heart

She lied
Thwarting this love
Leaving me desiccated and disenchanted
But no matter, sweet lady
For with every tick of the clock
This pool of darkness within rises
And will continue to
Till it pours from my mouth and eyes
As black the sin that tarnishes your saccharine spirit
An ocean
Which will consume all in its path

Pamela Morris
Con Fuoco

Each gray, barefooted step stirred up a rustle of dust,
a drop of rain on a dirt road, silent silt of movement.
The house is muted, smothered in the thick fog that rises
to meet the clouds after every storm.
Has it ever been so still before in the dreams?

The gauzy hallway stretches out, choked in layers of cobwebs,
a haunted, hunted ethereal existence.
My hand moves along the rail of the waist high wainscoting,
drawing a line,
disturbing that which will only settle down again behind me.

So very, very quiet.
Even the roar of the ocean seems to have stopped.
It no longer crashes and tears at the foundation.
Is this only a lull or has the storm truly passed?

Another page turns far down the foggy hallway.
It's him, of course, locked behind one of those doors.
Drab, paint-chipped, creaking, neglected doors,
The soft crinkle of each page matching the slow tread of my footsteps.

Which door? Can I remember which one?
So long since I put him there, locked him away to wait.
Locked away his eyes.
Locked away the power he holds over me.
Locked away what he offered.
The dream-nightmare he could make come true.
Too afraid. Too weak.
Teardrop on a musty carpet.

Here, this is the one.
Quivering shadows dance under the door,
another page turns.
My palm, flat on the scratchy painted surface.
The key itches in my hand,
slips into place, clicks.
So long,
I stand there until it feels like I too am covered with dust,
> gray cobwebs, hair gone white,
> hands cold, bloodless, stiff.

A husk stands at the door.
A roll of thunder now would shake the pillars into a mound of soot.
The faintest breath would scatter these ashes I have become.
My papery eyelids close.
The knob turns in my hand.

Covered with his music,

sheets and sheets, flutter, crinkle, scatter across the floor.
Every color faded to soft, mute dusty version of itself.
Ivory keys, tipped and rippled on top of a pile of broken green wood.
The lace curtains,
the table – still set with china and molded fruit,
the fireplace mantel,
draped in this thick, horrid death-gauze.

My heart sinks, knots, trembles as I move in closer.
There,
Resting in the chair, half out of its case,
his instrument,
his voice, his caress,
his soul.
Mute, choked like everything else,
Strangled into silence.

Warm in my hands,
Warm and silky smooth like his touch
When he slipped his fingers into mine ages ago.
My breath blows the dust away,
Blows back to the surface the dark grains of wood
                and rich varnish.
Touches the strings,
the sensual curves and scroll-worked handle.
Don't stop until it glows,
hot, living, breathing
                instrument of the Devil.

Burn it to my chest in agony.
"Maestro?"
Voice mingling with the dust,
Tears spatter on the sheets of music under bare feet.
Statue still.
Arms locked around this, his voice, now silent,
weeping.

The motes I've stirred shift,
One footstep in the dust.
His hand draws it out of me,
away from my heart,
                away from my tears and embrace.
Brushing it against my cheek,
                Or was that his kiss? that flaming
touch?

Slow,
Each gray barefooted step stirring up a wave of dust.
and papers.
And the silent silt of movement as my skirt sweeps
the floor.
The house is mute, smothered in that thick, gray fog
                except for here, this single room,
                at the center of it all.
Where my life burns like a flame
and rises from the ashes of the past
to dance with him.

Fierce Warrior of the Left-Hand Path

Walked I alone that darkest night,
With little regard to the streets and alleys,
drawn by unseen, unheard, unknown longings,
to thee, to the devil's blood-drenched valleys.

Vile, they called thee. Evil, wretched,
Soul of night's blackest wrath.
Be thee not blind to his wickedness,
This fierce warrior of the left-hand path.

But deny thee I could not do,
No more than could I deny my own desires.
Brought to thy lips; my throat, my blood,
Enflamed me thee with thy darkest fires.

"My sweet," thou didst call me,
Tossing to my heart the palest crumbs thy hath,
Enough to keep my passions fed,
Oh, fierce warrior of the left-hand path.

Cried out to thee I did each night
as thou faded backwards into the shadows.
Weeping for my own, raging, wandering heart
as the sunlight touched green meadows.

Warned they me of thy cruelty,
Waved before mine eyes thy wicked ways
unsurpassed.

But nay, my heart would heed them not
against thee, fierce warrior of the left-hand path.

Step away, I hath but tried in vain,
To let the Divine my plight to hold.
But each time thou reachest out to touch mine heart,
As if by some unnamed god thou art told,

"Let not this one slip away,
Let not this flower turn to shattered glass.
From she thou may need to feed one night,
Merciless, fierce warrior of the left-hand path."

"Oh, Love," screamed I. "Be thee patient.
Blind me not nor cover my ears with thy fiendish designs.
My heart can nay endure such pain
as to lose thee before thou art even mine!"

Bliss t'would be to rest in thy embrace,
Despite the warnings I've heard en masse.
We canst not help when we are driven by love
towards fierce warriors of the left-hand path.

I waited for thee to free thyself
of other worldly, ominous woes,
And come to me when thou couldest be free,
When thy darkest hour goes.

Seek me where thou knowest I to be,

Reach out, my knight, as tenderness defeats the wrath,
I shall embrace thee with a shining, sweet heart
For you, my fierce warrior of the left-hand path.

But came thee not to beckon me,
For all the long, weary obsidian nights I had waited.
Cold and misty fog tucked 'round my shivering shadow,
I believed them not, thy enemies, the Hated.

Longing, desire, heated, yearnings,
For the merest touch of the death-chilled hand thou hath.
Just one whisper, one caress, one tender glance,
From thee, I plead, fierce warrior of the left-hand path.

Walk I alone this darkest night,
With little regard to the streets and alleys,
Withdrawn to my despondent longings,
From thee, from the devil's cold, dead valleys.

Vile, thou art. Evil, wretched
emptier of my soul with thy blackest, sweetest breath.
Reaped was I by my blindest followings
for a fierce warrior of the left-hand path.

Brandon Ryals

The Kiss

Softly the rain falls as I sit alone
The light of the fire making shadows dance
Thunder rumbles as I watch her come to me
So beautiful, this creature before me
Her hair falls around her shoulders, a living waterfall
So soft the touch of her hand upon my chest, breathtaking is her smile
Transfixed by this enchantress I surrender to her
Close your eyes, place your faith in me, my love, she whispers
My body trembles at her touch, slowly her fingers trace the contours of my arms before taking my hands in hers
Inhaling deeply, I become intoxicated by her body's scent, my inhibition flees as her lips touch my throat
She guides my hands, exploring her body as her lips brush mine
Open your eyes, allow me to see you, she whispers
Yes, mistress, I say as I gaze into her eyes
Transfixed by the intensity of her stare, lost to the smouldering fires that burn into my soul
Tell me your desires, she whispers, show me your darkest fantasies and I will give you all you desire
Pleasure, I whisper, give me pain, show me how exquisitely evil you can be
I gasp as her teeth pierce my flesh, as she drinks from me
As you wish, my love, she whispers, close your eyes and embrace your darkness

My heart beats faster, threatening to burst from my chest
Endorphins flood my body as her nails tear into my flesh
Blood flows freely as our body's merge into one creature born from a primal lust
The heat between us rages into an inferno of forbidden passion
She begs me to taste her, forcing my mouth upon her throat
Moans of pleasure escape as I feed upon her, nothing so sweet as this forbidden nectar
Her smile so intoxicating as she licks the blood from my chin
Fierce the kiss that steals my breath as my hands become entangled in her hair
The sweat dripping from her brow mixes with the blood upon my lips
So deliciously wicked is the final moment shared, my body aches for release the fire within her becomes more than I can bear
My cries echo into the darkness as I collapse broken and spent
Yet for the price of such pleasure is paid in pain and soothed by her gentle kiss

Love's Damnation

So warm, the breath on my back
Soft is the touch upon my neck
I can feel her smile as she kisses me softly
Tell me what you desire, she whispers
Let me be your fantasy if only for this one night
My body trembles as her nails run down my spine
A sigh escapes me as she runs her tongue behind my ear
So sweet, the taste of your flesh, she says
Why do you torment yourself, my love
Surrender to me, allow me to satisfy your desires
Slowly I turn to face her, taking her in my arms
So calming is the touch of this creature before me
Do not fear me, I will not harm you, I could never hurt you, my love
Why have you come to me after all these years?
Why do you torment me so?
My vision blurred by tears, my heartbeats echo in my ears
Please forgive me, I have come so far to see you
I beg of you let me be yours, I surrender to you
My heart aches for her love, my soul in anguish as I pull away from her
She implores me, begs of my forgiveness
Close your eyes, place your hand in mine
She smiles so lovingly, her lips brush mine as I slide the blade into her heart
Know my pain, I whisper as she gasps
A smile forms as I gaze into her eyes
The look of pain and betrayal as at last she falls to the floor
Nothing so sweet as love's damnation

Sorrow's Kiss

Snow falls silent from an ashen sky
So enchanting, the blanket that covers the world around me
Cold reaches out to steal away the lingering warmth
As I sit here trying in vain to remember why I came to this place
It is the whisper in my ear that brings me back to reality
So cold the touch of her hand
Give into me and your pain will become a fading memory
So tempting to give in, to find warmth in her embrace
I can't surrender to her despite the bitter cold I try to fight
It is the subtle laughter that tells me I am doomed
Tears fall at the realization of my fate
Left here to wither a dying flower, I open my arms to her
Peace comes to me within the reaper's embrace

Heartache

So soft the tears that fall into darkness
Lost forever trapped within the ether
Love lays dying, scared and alone
Left here in solitude she grows cold
So bright the fire that burned within
Long since extinguished by sorrow
The heart withers a dying flower
No longer caring to fight the darkness
Shadows fall upon her enclosing her in a stygian darkness
Entombed by a primal force of eternal sadness, love begins to transform
Seeds of sorrow blooming into a bouquet of thorny hatred
Yet even amongst the stony soil of her heart, a single ember survives
Fanned by the winds of perdition it grows stronger
Where love's flame withered and died
A creature most deliciously wicked is born from the ashes
Behold the darkness of rage born from loves sacrifice

My Depression

Sitting here lost, trapped by the demons in my head,
I cry out in anguish
They pull me deeper into the darkness of my
depression, drowning me in emotions
That are too much to bear
Laughter echoes through the empty corridors as I
search for salvation
Tears of sorrow fall into the abyss as the realization
hits me
There is no escape from this hell of my own
creation
My only comfort, the demons that dwell within
For they are the only ones that love me
They have been with me forever and shall
Never leave

David Whippman
Hard History Lesson

She always argued when I used to say
We were like the great lovers of the past.
That was just woolly thinking, she'd insist:
Each separate period of history
Was quite different from us in the way
They defined romance. So my exotic list –
Caesar and Cleopatra and the rest –
Had no relevance for the present day.

She left me. There's not much I understand.
I stared for ages at our photographs;
They seem remote as long-ago events.
Her letters, now, seem hard to comprehend,
Indecipherable as hieroglyphs.
I'm no historian: none of this makes sense.

Hollywood Divorce

When it was obvious things weren't working out

(neither of us good on the other's cue)

of course we tried to talk. But I mean
we just weren't *scriptwriters*. Still... this nomination!

Yes, the role was cathartic.
I have to thank the director, for knowing
Exactly how much grief to cut.
Sacrifice for art? You bet! All the times
I woke crying in the night
And there were no cameras.

Frank Coffman
Residual Murder

I bought the old house for—as they say—"a song."
The old man was quite eager for the sale.
And there begins the weirdness of my tale.
For soon I knew that something was quite wrong.

I saw her first, then saw him with the knife
She ran toward me, rushing through the room—
Fleeing from him who planned to be her doom—
This ghost who sought to kill his pretty wife.

When they ran *through me*, I had to catch my breath.
I turned to see her trapped against the wall,
Cornered, he stabbed her heart! I saw her fall.
I saw her gasp her last, I saw her death!

Her sad eyes, as they dimmed, looked full at me!
In my own eyes the tears welled up and burned.
And then the husband wiped his blade—and turned.
I recognized the face! For it was he
Who'd sold the house, so eager to be rid
Of the place that witnessed his horrific act,
Of the ghostly replay that relived the fact,
Of the other scene that showed where she was hid!

For this grim spectacle repeated many nights,

And I could naught but watch again and again
And see her fear, and see her scream of pain!
But other acts were fixed in haunting sights:
I'd see them argue, see him strike her face;
I'd see her weeping there when he was gone;
I'd feel her anguish, as she pined alone.

But I'd also seen him make a hiding place!—
Open a space behind the bedroom wall,
Conceal her corpse in canvas, soaked in oil,
Smiling when he had finished that damned toil,
Believing he had concealed his crime from all.
All this I saw—and then I made a plan:
Somehow to bring the justice he was due
I asked the neighbors if, by chance, they knew
Of the young woman who had wed the man
Who owned the house before I took possession?
"She left him. That's what I heard," said the one.
"Went home to Boston, left him for another."
"I heard she took up with that poor man's brother!"
Another said. "She was a pretty thing
And turned men's heads wherever she would go.
Where she went off to no one seems to know."
"I noticed he took off his wedding ring,"
Said one. One lady said, "I have a confession.
I can't help thinking that he might have killed her!
I know that's crazy talk, but, just the same,
There were suspicions and the police came
'Round one day and looked about the place
And questioned him, but they could find no trace
Of her. And them so lately wed!"

No reason to doubt the tale that she had fled,
Gone off in her young lust with someone new,
Gone to with no one knew, nor whither to.

I had to act. The ghostly dramas played
Now every night in that old, cursed place
I couldn't keep from looking at that face
That gazed in repeated death throes straight at me.
Justice for her had been too long delayed.
I had to set her troubled spirit free!

Left in the cellar with old furniture,
The monster had cast aside an oval frame
With rounded glass that held a fair picture
Of the beautiful young girl who took his name.

My plan was simple: When the police came 'round
To see the horror that I said I'd found
Behind the bedroom wall. "The plaster failed
While hanging that pretty picture. As I nailed
The hanger into place, the hammer went
Clear through the wall, and then I caught the scent
Of something wrong, the clear smell of decay,"
I'd said. "I pulled more chunks away. Dear God!
I called you when I saw what lay behind
That cursed wall. I hope that you can find
Whoever did this!"

                      "Don't worry on that score,"
One officer soon said. "I'm sure I know
Whose body you have found—who did this crime—

Beautiful Tragedies - A Dark Poetry Anthology

And we have had suspicions for some time.
There's really nowhere the old man can go,
I've got men even now outside his door."

Just then he looked down at the oval frame,
Sitting upon the chair. "It's weirdly just,"
He said. "You finding her as you hung
Her picture."
                    I asked, "What was her name?"
"Wasn't she beautiful? Her name was Grace,"
He answered. "Well, she's forever young
In this old photo."
                    Smiling at that face,
We each held back a tear.

. . . . .

                    But I must
Finish my strange tale. That very night
There was no repeat of the murder scene,
Nor any of the other sad vignettes.
Perhaps even a house of horror forgets
If things are somehow changed from what has been,
If things are somehow, some way set aright?

But one last ghostly vision came that day
(Believe or disbelieve it matters not.)
Grace came and smiled at me and turned away.
That smile she gave shall never be forgot.

I sold the house for much less than I paid.

A place of murder hasn't much appeal.
I'm happy in the new home I have made
In a different town—surrounded by *the Real*.
But often this strange story I recall
As I smile at the oval portrait on the wall.

Phil Wolters
Ruminations of Death while Stopped at a Traffic Light in Calgary

I'm stopped here in red light traffic surrounded by the exhaust clouds.
The cars are all tan, black, and grey; they've forgotten to be colourful.
We're all on our way to somewhere, going to get something done.
It just seems like every day we spend is like every other one.

And in this moment, we're alive.
We don't even have to try.
We just wait and pass the time
At this and many other lights.

The light finally changes, and the cars can now start on their way
To appointments and interviews, meetings and massages, car washes and first dates.
Nothing is different on this grey weekday in early spring.
Nothing is different here, except maybe for everything.

Suddenly I feel alive
Stuck in traffic on this drive.
I know that it won't last for long

Before this journey of life is done.

It's a change that we all could use while waiting for our lives to begin.
We sleepwalk through all our days, alive yet we forget to live.
Until one day you wake up old and over, wishing for that time again.
Looking back on those wasted moments, wishing you'd made more time for sins.

The same thing's waiting for us all
As sure as winter follows fall.
One day we draw our final breath
And embrace that last release of death.

Live well or not, it's up to you.
But remember that no matter what you do,
No matter if you're great or lame
Everyone's story ends the same.

Charles Gramlich
One Recipe for Disaster

A soupcon of cryptic argument
One too many late-night calls
A single silken hair from Venus

Mix with snark and venom
Allow to set

Bake fifteen minutes in the
glare of a spoiled child

Serve hot

Stained

Lying stained in the evening,
like a forgotten god,
a hateful thing with lips
that promise nothing.

In the final hour of day,
when blood red sky
dies to black night,
he opens bruised eyes.

Away in the shadows,
from a world that seethes,
comes a scrawl of beetles,
a gathering of worms.

He parts lips and smiles,
awaiting the empty cloak
that will at last
dress him in love.

Crown of Flies

In the embers of a dream,
pale with hoarfrost,
her eyes give glory to the night.

Tears sing from the darksouls
that crouch at her shoulders,
stain the silks she wears like rags.

The litter of death fills her mouth.
The kiss of fear rides her tongue.
She sews her cloak from beetle wings
and hate.
She paints her lips with sin.

From her lover's blood,
she bakes fine rubies
to decorate necklace and crown,
the necklace of lives,
the crown of flies.

And when she carves poetry
into the pages of my skin,
she will be happy,
she will be sated,
she will be mine.

Denise Jury
Scarred Heart

You touched my heart
Left a mark
Time has moved on
The scar remains

Haiku 1

Damage has been done
Your hand has torn my heart out
Love bleeding away

Haiku 2

Your voice is a dream
I hear it in the daytime
A waking nightmare

Haiku 3

There is a coldness
It's settled into my heart
You left it in me

Haiku 4

I once saw the stars
When I looked into your eyes
Now there is darkness

Ryan Woods
Bleed, Bitch, Bleed

Drip…
Drop…
Drip…
Drop…
I told you that one day I would put a stop
to your cheating, and your lies.
I grew to despise
your very existence.
Resistance
was futile
Pure thoughts, and puerile ambitions
lay butchered and bleeding
Your screams, and your pleading,
only succeeded
in sealing your fate.
Too little…
Too late…
I found the key
to release me,
and now the gloves are off.
You created a monster,
and now a dumpster
will be your final resting place.
You destroyed my worth,
so, I destroyed your face.
You were once as pretty as a picture,
but you're no oil painting, anymore.

Crawling,
you almost made it to the door
before I dragged you,
kicking and screaming
into your own nightmare.
Fair's, fair
One good deed deserves another.
So, your lover
is next
I took your phone,
and sent him a text
"Come on over, I'm horny", I wrote,
pretending to be you.
And like a puppy,
he came running.
What a cunning
stunt.
The cunt
never saw me coming
From the darkness,
I emerged, like a demon…
"Dream on", I said
as I put the gun to his head,
and sent him to meet his maker
The Lord giveth,
and the Lord taketh away
You even tried to pray
for forgiveness,
begging like a dog
But, once the black fog
began descending,

a sticky ending
was all that was waiting for you
I stood by you, through thick and thin,
but I finally wiped the grin
from your face.
You were a disgrace
to the vows that we once took.
So, FUCK you!!
I may have blood on my hands,
but I finally feel cleansed.
I made mistakes,
but now I've made amends.
And so, I bid you farewell.
I may go to hell
for my deeds,
but needs must.
So,
Ashes to ashes
and
Dust to dust.

Humble Pie

The only thing that you ever baked for me
was Humble Pie,
which you served cold, like revenge.
But, in the end
vengeance was mine.
I built a shrine,
at which to worship you,
like an idol.
But a tidal wave of deceit,
was how you repaid me.
Life with you
was a tropical storm
I would count the seconds
after the thunder,
and wonder
when the lightning
would strike.
You were the shrike,
that impaled me
upon my own good will.
Yet, still
I came back for more.
You took pleasure
in making me your whore
You fucked with my head,
and now you lie dead
at my feet,
wrapped in a sheet,

and bound with string.
I no longer, long for anything.
My requests for you to cease and desist
always fell on deaf ears
So, I took the garden shears,
and vented my rage
I released the beast
from its cage,
and now the least that you can do,
is to give me some peace.
Rest in Pieces.
You always liked to put yourself around
So, now you can be found,
here,
and there,
chunks of my past
wrapped up like gifts.
No if's
No and's
No but's
You had the last word
But I had the last laugh
Perhaps that should be my epitaph?

Slipknots and Razorblades

I stuck my neck out for you,
and in return you handed me a noose
So, I have decided it is time to cut you loose.
I do not want to hang with you anymore.
There's the door.
Don't let it hit you in the ass as you leave.
I may have taken leave of my senses,
jumped through hoops
and scaled fences for you.
But, those days are gone.
You are just one,
of the many mistakes that I have made,
for which I have paid the price.
You fed me a slice
of reality,
and now I am sick to my stomach
of your condescending ways,
your mind games,
and your power plays.
You think that it is funny,
treating me the way that you do.
But I will humour you,
No More.
You treat me like a whore,
thinking that you can fuck with me
whenever you see fit.
But now the shit
has hit the fan

and I can't understand
how you can be so blind
to find me guilty
of any crime.
If I had a dime
for every time
that I allowed you to take advantage of me,
I would be rich
beyond my wildest dreams.
It seems,
that no good deed goes unpunished,
and I am serving hard time for mine.
You handed me down a life sentence
when you said, "I do".
If I only knew
Then,
what I know
Now.
Oh, how different things would be.
I am only human.
If you cut me I bleed,
and you seem to feed
on my pain.
You are a razor blade,
that leaves scars on the surface,
and deep inside.
But there is a place where I can hide,
when everything becomes too much.
Such is the beauty of my imagination.
It bears no relation
to the reality of the situation

that I find myself in.
I can be whatever I want to be.
I can be a wolf, roaming free
across an Arctic tundra.
I sit here,
and wonder,
where you would be
if I had not intervened
in the nightmare
that you once were living.
I did all the Giving,
and you did all the Taking.
Forsaking my trust.
Now dust,
and ghosts
are the only hosts
to the celebration
of our union.
Even a holy communion
cannot exorcise
the demons
that your lies
have created.
I waited
for Love,
and Hated
every minute
of what you gave
me instead.
You got inside my head,
and rearranged all the cogs,

every nut
and every bolt;
finding fault
with everything that I do,
and everything that you see.
Fool me once,
Shame on you...
Fool me twice,
Shame on me...

The Start of the End is only Half the Story

Some things never tarnish, such is their purity
Even honey that has crystalized with age,
can be revitalized with warmth,
as many things can.
But love…
When love starts to die,
you may as well turn off the life support machine
There's no coming back from an edge that's
as cold as an arctic wind
and as unforgiving
as a switchblade
So, you listen to the last few blips
of the life, it once had
grow weaker,
and then flatline,
in the same way that you felt the warmth
drain from it.
Then say goodbye
And allow it passage
to that place where all things that are broken beyond repair
must go.
There will be tears.
There always is when something dies,
but better to let go
than to reach for rainbows that will never materialize
from the storm that you've been trying to ride out
Time to hang up your saddle,

else be a rodeo rider clinging on to hope
and the rope,
thinking that if you can stay on
for just a few more seconds, the buzzer might sound
And victory will be yours.
But there are no victors in this war
No champions, no heroes, just casualties.
Broken hearts, tormented minds, tortured souls
"Abandon all hope, ye who enter here" wrote Dante
And abandon it, we do.
Hope is for those misguided in the belief
that life is fair,
that the good guy always wins,
that the dice aren't weighted in the casino's favour
And that good deeds bring with them
just rewards.
Realists, realize that no good deed
goes unpunished
Save someone from an abusive marriage,
only to in turn, be abused by them,
Payback is a bitch.
They say that violence begets violence.
I guess that you felt it fair for abuse to beget abuse
And so, you set about making
me pay
for someone else's crimes.
You didn't care who paid.
just so long as someone did,
and more often than not,
I was the one who stood in the firing line
when you pulled the trigger.

Ill equipped to protect myself,
I had no flak jacket to shield me from
your poisonous slurs.
Soaking up every name,
every insult,
every accusation
that you spat at me,
like a sponge that had been anointed with
Holy Water
to give it a fighting chance
against the demons
Waking each morning, wondering
if storm clouds
are going to start gathering throughout the day,
your armchair becomes the electric chair
and you sit there, and wait
to ride the lightning.
Sometimes lightning strikes more than once.
From hero to zero,
in the blink of an eye.
Slain by a green-eyed monster,
who would not listen to reason.
Too wrapped up in their own selfishness,
like a present that never starts giving
and never stops taking.
The best years of your life lay behind you,
lost in a haze.
The worst years lay ahead,
waiting to add insult to injury,
in the same way
that some people do.

There is no use in prospecting for gold,
once you've come to realize that iron pyrite
is your lot in life.
This was never going to be a tale of Hope and Glory,
The Start of the End is only Half the Story.

Love's Last Breath

I know that you do not really love me.
I have come to accept that,
as I have come to accept my own mortality,
Begrudgingly.
Did you ever?
Perhaps.
Back when you saw me as a Knight
in shining armour,
your dreams, made flesh…
Or was I always just the skeleton key,
that you used to pick the lock
on the cell,
that you found yourself languishing in?
You watched me through the bars
of your matrimonial hell,
having marked off the days
of your life
that you had wasted,
before I came along.
In the wake
of your prison break,
that I was an accomplice to,
you wasted no time in spreading your wings,
and tasting the things
that you had previously been denied.
But our relationship became a landslide
of bad decisions and bad choices
We raised our voices,

and you raised your hand
But you could never understand
why I never hit back
Drowning in this loveless relationship
There is no life preserver
You said that you loved me,
but nothing could be further
from the truth.
MURDERER!!
You strangled our relationship
with your bare hands
and now it lies rotting,
like a corpse
in a shallow grave.
I thought that marriage would be a pleasure cruise,
but you turned it into a shipwreck
And so, I stand on deck
and watch as a storm rolls in…
Sink or swim,
seem to be my only choices
So, I close my eyes
and briefly wonder,
before allowing the voices
in my head to drag me under.

Richard Alan Long
A Martyr for the Brokenhearted

Joy division playing Love will tear us apart
On a train journey filled with war and peace
Echoes and images of my past life in glorious Technicolor
Gazing at my reflection and feeling romantic disgust
Discovering new scars just as the old ones heal
Smell of freshly cut grass in the summer air
Joy division playing Love will tear us apart
Sunday dinners in hot stuffy rooms
Watching with disinterest old John Wayne movies
Trying to find sleep but finding sleep won't find me
Seeing her face electric and unfeeling
Wanting to phone friends who no longer care
Punching the walls until my knuckles scream with feeling
Joy division playing Love will tear us apart
Making progress but sinking in the sentimental snow
Having fucked up nightmares of us together in fucked up places
Wondering how much damage a soul can actually take
Wishing that I could become more mechanical like everyone else
Hearing her name and wanting to be part of it
Joy division playing Love will tear us apart

I've Got My Summer Right Now

I loved her until my eyes stung
She could sing dance and create
She could do anything
She always had this amazing ability
To smile away all my blues

I watched her drown peacefully
I held her hand tenderly
Sound of a carnival over my shoulder
The smell of her sweat on my neck
Her kicking feet across my shins

I let go of her locked fingers
I kissed them one by one
And sensed a single beat of her heart
Black mascara unfocused eyes watching me
Looking up through me at the summer sky

I walked away looking at the dirty ground
Dead scarlet leaves wet and stuck to my boots
Someone far away shouts for a second chance
Music filled the air with images of her face
And I can't help but think
She'd never looked this beautiful

The Woman at the Window

There's a woman at my bedroom window
She's been watching me for weeks
Every night she comes to see me
She has pallid skin and violet lips
Her hair is the colour of Autumn leaves
It sticks to her face, wet and claw like

She comes up from the ground at night
roams the graves for her belongings
She asks if I think she looks pretty
I am scared so I always say yes
She smiles with teeth as black as the sky
She tells me tales of her man far away

I told my parents and they left silently
Every night dad stands at my window
My mother is worried and worn
After several days, my parents give up
They tell me the nightmares must have passed
Until one night she returned

She smiled a joyless smile
I saw her eyes flooded with tears
I don't know why but I opened the window
I wanted to show them she wasn't a dream
Her hands clamped to my throat cold and stinging
She whispered to me her name
She said she never got the chance to feel love

My parents found me on my bedroom floor
We swapped rooms and they slept in my place
One night when the sky was dark I heard my dad shouting
My mother was crying and saying it was a mistake
I shout for them and all was silent
My dad came to me and gripped me so tight
Told me he'd love me forever

In the morning, I walked to my room
The door was ajar so I went inside
The bed was empty and the window open
Downstairs my mum was cooking breakfast
She has pallid skin and violet lips
Her hair is the colour of Autumn leaves
It sticks to her face, wet and claw like
She asked me if I thought she looked pretty
I am scared so I say yes

James Longmore
No One Dies Instantly

'He was dead before he hit the ground,'
They say.
'He didn't know what hit him,'
They say.
'At least it was quick,'
They say.
But death comes no quicker to one man over another,
As every brain will take its own sweet time to die
Give or take.
Shot, stabbed, strangled, drowned, smothered,
Suicide bomb, blown asunder, head popped like a champagne cork,
Imagine what wondrous thoughts they must experience as they fly through the air?
Six minutes - six whole, entire and complete minutes before the brain begins its decent into the black inevitability of death,
And three minutes after that to give up its ghosts, one by tortuous one.
Nine minutes in all, to contemplate and to think,
To realize that death is no more than those nine short minutes away.
Listening to the hollow quiet of your heart,
No longer beating its comforting, familiar rhythmic tattoo,

Lungs stilled, dead air growing warm and stale inside,
Stinking gas expelled, mercifully unable to inhale and smell the stench of one's own demise.
A body stilled, silent.
Waiting for that bright, white light of myth to come along,
The glorious tunnel to loved ones and eternal salvation.
But it does not visit this lost and lonely soul.
All goes black, so terribly and finally and irrevocably black,
To be followed by consciousness, thoughts, behaviors learned across a brief lifetime, cut so cruelly short by the hand of another,
'It's like dreaming,'
They say.
Last to go, after memories, emotions and all that has been learned,
And thinking; I *don't* think; therefore, I am not.
Hearing; the detection of sound, immaterial now as not so much as a heartbeat may be heard.
For now, there is nothing.
And so,
I lie down beside you and wonder what you are thinking.

Brandy Delight
The Final Filter

I saw the guilt behind your eyes, bloodshot maps of lies and betrayal dry, pursed lips afraid to speak; the cat got the tongue of a liar. I felt you tremble when you held me, goose bumps and curled fingertips, your grasp is frail, weak and soft, and the monkey on your back weighs on you. I smelled the fear on your stench, the wretched bouquet, illness of coward, essence of sewage, lust and urge, sweating bullets must blister hide. I filtered out your fairytales, straining foul love through mesh and lace, tossing away the wilted flowers you gave, dancing with the skeletons in your closet. I gave up on you, my lover, my friend, long before another shared our cradle, when our hearts conjoined in forever, a heart is strong in its weakest time, now walk away, although alone I cry, you meet with delusion and like leaving you is hard to swallow, choking; an idle love is the devil's playground.

Wedding Vows

When you chose alcohol over love, you wrote your obituary, rather than your wedding vows. You welcomed a new bartender into your life, rather than a blushing bride. Your body has been embalmed by a Happy Hour mortician. Bloodshot eyes peer through yellowing lenses. Your body is pickled, like an aborted fetus in a jar. You embraced beer like a mistress, tenderly tasting its familiar nectar, every night before fitful rest, then kissing the morning sun, with whiskey on your breath, you take your bottle of self-confidence, wherever you may squander, confessing all your dirty little secrets, to Mr. Daniels riding shotgun, in conspiracy to commit rebellious DUI. You expel your liver, in one jaundice, bloody clot after another, vomiting, retching, and sobbing, then taking another drink, to wash the bile from your throat. Your hand should have been cradled in mine, instead of double fisting micro brews. So, you bid me fare thee well, choosing alcohol over love. Continuing your sordid love affair, with pale ale, and a bottle of Beam; writing your obituary, rather than your wedding vows.

Ancient Friend

Rely on the strength of strangers, for friends will always let you fall. I would incline you to look me in the eyes, while spitting lies in my face, rather than tripping me when my back is turned. Cowards crucify the strong, they fear what they do not understand. You cling to me like a summer shadow. An ignorant fledgling, unable to fly. But my nest is full of truth, and your feathers are still down, useless fluff, useless friend.

Rely on the kindness of strangers, their loyalty is free. As I revolt, I hold the hand of the nameless. Together we are empowered by mutual anarchy, pushing against the current of wishful thinking. We swim upstream in a combustible waterfall, as you my friend, hold the life line selfishly. You narcissistic, egomaniac, watch me drown. Unattached to reality, you are uncomplicated, a common washed out wasteland. I find my breath from under the waves, as you squirm like a fish out of water.

Rely on the love of strangers, an ally for a night, without promised tomorrows, and a subtle allegiance through a blind man's gaze. We share knowledge and memories, without passable judgment and dagger glares. We can touch without cringing resentment. You always pull away from my eager embrace. Arms of friendship do not break, rather envelope one in unconditional cover. But history has hoarded bricks and mortar. Secrets for the grave, spilled with loose tongue. Intoxicated betrayal from an ancient friend.

Forrest J Hiler
Six

Rounds locked into place,
One by one.
Each is placed into position,
Patiently waiting.
Chambered in perfect design,
Singing terrors.
A melody of prayers harmonizing,
All in peace.
A simple number calls out,
Three letters.

One is too low to be significant,
Ringing dully against a bell.
Two is larger but still too silent,
Bouncing off bone in humor.
Three is halfway there but quiet,
Rising in volume with tears.
Four is a magical euphoric melody,
Vibrating the mirror to pieces.
Five sing volumes with a concerto,
Counting to the final show.
Six yells a symphony of horror,
Telling you to be silent again.

One is left empty and spent,
Vacant lot here.
Two is discarded towards the floor,

Business closed sign.
Three is without a second glance,
Sold out, sorry.
Four is removed and tossed aside,
Sorry, try again later.
Five is voided out of commission,
Come back tomorrow.
Six is loaded and raring to go,
Flip a coin.

The spinning silences my voice,
A final question passes by:
"Do you believe in second chances?"

...Trigger pulled, hammer falls, the gavel sounds...

Pull the Trigger

Barrel pressed to my forehead,
I stare my assailant down.
My own reflection brought to life,
Holding a six-shooter steady.
My eyes lock with my own grey eyes,
A glare meets a sneer.
Risking everything and more right now,
I press the barrel closer.
Sweat and tears flooding both of me,
Solemnly both whisper:
"Pull the trigger right here and now,
We'll see who's the strongest.
Either way neither of us wins this war,
There will be no victor.
Only one love sick loser in a pine box,
With a fleeting moment."
I feel the heat from my own blood flow,
Swallowing my own sick pride.
I bellow at my own reflection in agony,
"PULL THE DAMN TRIGGER!"

Nothing happens for a moment,
I look up at my reflection holding the gun.
He's struggling to keep his grip,
Fear and insecurity slowly set in his face.
I press the barrel to my skull harder,
Glaring back in absolute rage and hatred.

Tears and sweat causing the gun to slip,
"C'mon, do us a favor and pull the trigger.
We don't have all day to wait,
You want this war to end, don't you?"
My reflection squirms and refocuses grip,
Determination fills his eyes.
"You know you want to end this pain,
All this agony and suffering.
End it, be free of it, stop resisting,
SO, GO AHEAD AND PULL THE TRIGGER!"

Nothing happens again,
And I realize that I am not the hatred.
I am the reflection,
Struggling to understand my war.
I thought I fought alone,
Little did I see I never fought in isolation.
I always fought against myself,
But I was unsure and insecure of my choices.
So now as I stare myself down,
I realized that I am the only loser in this war.
Frustrated and confused,
I throw the gun away from me and my hatred.
My war will not claim me,
I have too much work to do and so much to see.
My darkness fades back,
Merging back into the me that is whole.
I often have to stifle his voice,
Constantly whispering softly in my ear:
"C'mon...Just pull the trigger."

Twisted Mentality

Imagine with me friends,
A corruption of minds.
Warped beyond all repair,
Mad by the very nature.
Crippled by failed words,
Unable to speak clearly.
Agony creeps in the veins,
Facilitating a dark room.
Deep inside the shadows,
Battles rage forever more.
What monstrous creations,
Lurk within a twisted mentality?

Laughter resounds and echoes peacefully,
Disturbing the very marrow of your bones.
Doors with locks line the hallways forever,
However, there are no hinges to hold them.
Windows illuminate all dimly from the moon,
Showing you the very passive writings on walls.
Spiders fill the air in swarms of fearful motions,
Suffocating the very light that once was there.
Corners rise from the floor erratically upwards,
Reaching for a ceiling that seemingly isn't there.
Chains fall from the sky of nothingness,
Grasping towards you with empty desires.
Jagged are the stairs of the hospital,
Bouncing up and down with childish glee.
Forbid I ask you to move forward,

Unless you want to discover a twisted mentality.

Behold the one room with actual candlelight,
Black flames give off a white ghastly glow.
Vibrant colors flow from the gate that lies before,
What do you wish to see from the prismatic madness?
Unicorns, Dragons, Demons and Angels all fly forth,
Yet die off when they leave the glow of light.
A child's voice echoes in your mind,
"Please release me from my torment."
Waves of emotion flood the corridor,
As desperation sets quickly in your skull.
"Please release me from my prison,"
Pleas continue to ring out from your own lips.
Silence eludes you as terror sets in your soul,
"Please release me from my pain," it screams!
Tears fall from the heavens,
Crashing with the weight of anvils!
"PLEASE RELEASE ME FROM MY CURSE!"
The voice wails in your mind and from you.
Ropes fly from the walls with a dark purpose,
To subdue and restrain the escapee's wrists.

Stillness sets in your shattered mind,
Realizing you are the escapee and are trapped.
A lone figure approaches you,
Holding a clear vial and the syringe of silence.
"Please release me from captivity,"
Your empty plea seeks open ears painfully.
Not a word is spoken to you,

A simple nod and a motion combining vial and syringe.

"Please release me from my insanity,"
A tearful plea escapes and falls upon deaf ears.
"Rest now. The nightmare is almost over,"
A simple response followed by a swift motion.
Needle punctures flesh and tears fall,
Liquid moves and flows in your veins filling your heart.
Darkness fills your vision and sleep follows,
Slumbering for what is an eternity...

Awake in your own room,
Peaceful winds blow softly.
A nightmare that plagued you,
Has now gone and passed.
Something is amiss though,
A new mark is on your arm.
Was it all a dream for you,
Or an elaborate illusion,
Created by your mind?

That is what it feels,
To have a twisted mentality.

Hades Rising
Underneath the Mourning Star
The Tragedy of God-Crossed Lovers

I spied Faith sitting upon a rail
Fair hair in the wind
Watching the ships set sail
Whispers from her wonder if
She'll ever see me again
As I sail off into the rift

Gone to fight in God's own war
Clad in celestial armor
I go to break the door
Of things so vile and beneath
Us, the holy army
We will crush them under our feet

> In Heaven, God looked upon Faith
> And saw that without me
> She was but a wraith
> And sadness filled His heart

Between the battles, I dream of her
Sitting there so lonely
Drawing her picture in the dirt
Falling leaves remind me of the time
Of splendors and apples
Before sin was a crime

> Here in His kingdom sat one so blind

To the love that shone
But then Faith was still mine
A forbidden affair in His home

In the heat of Battle I threw down their King
Their morale was broken
And enemy horde felt the sting
I proclaimed my victory for God's glory
And headed for home
To Heaven, to tell the story

    Word spread to the Lord of my win
    But He was full of envy
    For in His house Faith and I sinned
    In His eyes there were many

Sat her down in comfort
Then told her about my doom
She wept upon the shoulder of the Lord
But to him it was just
Another player knocked off the board

There she stood on top of the stairs
And the air was so thick with despair
Her stricken heart set to un-tune her
And grief poured forth to consume her
With one last pull of the heart strings
She cast herself from the spire
And the cold night air was lit up with fire

    God was then struck with a rage
    And barred me from the chamber floor
    I was to be condemned in a cage

And I looked into the face of mistrust
Once filled with just, but nevermore

"Cast me, Father, as you cast her out!
Throw me from your heart!"
And thus, I lashed about
"I have lost Faith to her doom!"
The, I, The Morningstar
Cursed God from Heaven to distant moons.

And He said:

"Her pride for you kept her so fair
Your death by my word led to despair
I cast you out, into the dark
Let the lash of her death leave a mark."

And so, I fell
Through fire and earth
To rule beneath
A new rebirth
And still I search
For where she burned
I have looked afar
From Hell to Earth
I am still The Mourning Star

Crimson Lips of Death

Her scarlet lips sucking, eagerly, on severed veins
Outlining the facts between predator and prey
An icon of Christ, the crucifix and rusted nails
I fall into her arms for a beautiful Hell

Kiss me with crimson lips
Kiss me with crimson lips of death

And drink from my wasted flesh
I feel the reaper's caress
Lost within the cold eclipse
Smothered in your deathly kiss

And pull me down
Into a winter burial

Goblets lined beneath candles filling with dark red wine
Draining virgins strung high dying less than divine
I sup from betwixt her breast like a new dead babe
Cradle me with cruelty, I am her willing slave

Kiss me with crimson lips
Kiss me with crimson lips of death

And drink from my wasted flesh
I feel the reaper's caress
Lost within the cold eclipse

Smothered in your deathly kiss

And pull me down
Into a winter burial

Dance for me beneath the full moon light
Like a wraith within the darkest night
I remember the epitaph
Scribed on her tomb
I remember the epitaph
Scribed
On
Her
TOMB

THESE WORDS ECHO SO GRIMLY
DEMONS INSIDE THE GRAVE
ARE CLAWING AT THE DIRT
BREAKING THROUGH THE SOIL AGAIN

Kiss me with crimson lips
Kiss me with crimson lips of death

And drink from my wasted flesh
I feel the reaper's caress
Lost within the cold eclipse
Smothered in your deathly kiss

And pull me down
Into a winter burial

Beautiful Tragedies - A Dark Poetry Anthology

Dance for me beneath the full moon light
Like a wraith within the darkest night

Splinter in the Heart

I take your picture from the box
And rest it in my weary hands
It's bringing memories to bear
So many what ifs and should haves
Are outweighed by promised tomorrows

I'll make it up to you
I swear
But now I never can

I see you every day in the mirror
And I can hear you even though you're not there
Because I've never seen it more clearer
You're gone
YOU'RE GONE
But I'm still here

Never meant to fail you so bad
I might've tried but not enough
Shattered myself to wish you back
But fate it seems to have deaf ears
Or perhaps it never cared at all

I'll make it up to you
I swear
But now I never can

I see you every day in the mirror

And I can hear you even though you're not there
Because I've never seen it more clearer
You're gone
YOU'RE GONE
But I'm still here

The splinter you left behind
Has worked its way deep in my heart
Ever since the day I stood
With our family beside the grave

I'll make it up to you
I swear
But now I never can

I see you every day in the mirror
And I can hear you even though you're not there
Because I've never seen it more clearer
You're gone
YOU'RE GONE
But I'm still here

So many stars in the sky
But I cannot seem to find you
Among so many I've lost
So, please, just shine brighter for me

Rana Kelly
Boy

six months
'til December again, boy...
did you know-
your face flashes
across my eyes
every day
and on that one, that day...
30th December-
one year
since you ran from me
it will rain.
i'll curl up
in a blanket
and let again your loss overtake me...
you could have just died, you know.
accident, murder, ill.
but you knew me too well, boy
you wear the outskirts
as do i.
our own personal
hand
me
down.
you decided
to keep my secret

without telling me.
you took it to the
place
you know
very well, boy
you know
very well i
want to look
you know
that
you and me
we have
that
skeleton key
to all of the doors
that all of those
are afraid to walk
through.
the thresholds
are dusted
with snow
and everyone
turns away
after they
lay the flowers
there
beneath
your name...
they don't have
the grip
the strength

to shoulder
the pain
and push past
the latch
on your heart
and mine.
and that's why, boy
that's why
they call it
winter.

For Ed Sluka Jr.

April 1975-December 2009

Carrion

Dead roses
And shriveled lust
You wiped
The blue dust
Off of my wings.
And now just
The ravens
Sing.
Carrion cries
Into the trees
Mountains of
Bones, fur
Teeth
And all manner
Of dead and broken
Things.

Wolves

my Wolves
cry out
on lonely nights.
but I
am not there
to hear them.

Jason Prenatt
King of Worms
Heironymus Bosch

I am a classic case of anti-social
trichotilomaniac
behavior suggests extreme stress,
surrounded by damaged perverts
this is my home
she is my fetishist queen
I am dominant top/bottom heretic
we inch our way below her feet
we eat dirt and shit out soil
we lick whatever we please
she lives with me inside our private transparent
sphere
we swim in the pool of debauchery
anti-eden we consume the serpent's fruit
her pleasure is my pleasure
master-slave-master
I want to hold her prenatal,
I want to sew her birth wounds,
induce her,
be the Alpha & Omega.
I want her surgical cesarean
I am her wet nurse majesty
she's my eternal patient
anti-psychotic, anti-everything
I read from the notes that appear to suggest sodomy
I play her body's symphony
Every note's composed from her breath
which I'm blessed to be in the presence of
She's crowned my head with cum

Where monarchy's a dirty word
What am I the king of?
I'm the king of worms

In Utero Cover Art
Kurt Cobain

Even vultures spread their wings in pride.
Metaphor for seahorse,
why can't I sing?
I carry your bloated uterus
catch your green & sore cord.
Macabre & menstrual
my auburn eyed antisexual,
my hermaphrodidtic Aphrodite,
I absorb the cells you shed.
Hymen high on rusted pedestal,
are you waiting for me?
Hold your hands out masochistic messiah.
I water your dried-out intestines,
I patch your skin.
My saliva is the glue
but I can swim through the tissue
& sink into the membrane,
incarcerate myself
somewhere between your ribs— my coffin.

Venus in Furs

She sits on me
I am her holy chair
she whips me with a switch
I am her favorite target
she shoots me with her Cupid arrow
I am her heart, her blood, her bone marrow
I am caught inside her scarlet hair
you can find me there braiding the locks
of my *maitresse*, my *sacher*

Paul Bridgeman
When I See You Again

When I see you again
When I saw you last week
It had been quite a while,
You still have that mad look,
There's that goofy smile,
You used to have a smile for me,
For a time, it was only mine,
But it made me forget the hurt,
I was glad to see you again,
I was glad we ripped the plaster off
Now it won't hurt so much when I see you again,
When I see you again,
I won't run if you don't see me,
When I see you again,
I won't feel your claws are still buried in me,
You look older now and I do too,
Your eyes are just the same though,
So very distant and oh so blue,
Our hair is thin and coloured,
And our past is too,
But we wouldn't change a thing,
The laughter and the pain,
The truth is that I would still leave you,
Glad it doesn't hurt so much seeing you again
When I see you again,
I won't run if you don't see me,

When I see you again,
I won't feel your claws are still buried in me,
But when we part a part of me will still be blue,
The part of me you once ripped in two

Burn!

In that time that looked so good,
From the outside at least,
I sat and smiled while the flames twisted,
And the house burned brightly,
Friends tried to drag me from the fire,
People said that I should put it out,
But I wanted to see,
I could see a future in flickering heat shimmer,
Through my smile I showed no pain,
Yet I felt it in my heart again then again,
I wanted to hold you to say no
But when that eye is open it will have its way,
And we were yin and yang so long,
I had to see your betrayal to believe it,
I had to feel this pain to recover,
I had to feel this pain so my love would not kill me,
And on the Eastern horizon a silhouette appeared,
And I burned and smiled but became invisible,
It was easier to watch through the flames now,
Through the lies and justification, I smiled,
You could not see that I did not need them,
I was watching you tear us apart,
You needed no help no approval,
The lovers arrived they could smell that you had gone,
I still watched but now I was not alone,
If I was to keep you I had to know it was true,
If you stayed without this test I could only hate you,

So I smile and burn inside show nothing,

And I watch the fool who was once my pride,
Ridden by another and drained of all resource,
Held below the waste and followed by your mind,
I would not fight for you or with you,
Like all Satan's, do what you will, shall be all of the law
As your sickness evaporated before me,
You thought I didn't see it as the fake it was,
And I smiled and I burned but more swiftly,
The lovers helped me with the burning,
A shell of flame a centre cooling,
I watch you magnify your worth,
No longer happy with achievement,
I watched you become desperate to be someone,
Unaware that no-one cared and all knew the lie,
LIAR! Liar! But it's me who is on fire,
You told me that no-one had ever called you a cunt,
I advised that was only to your face,
The flames flared and died and I could see you,
No flames no heat haze just a desperate man,
You needed control I did not give enough,
You needed love there was never enough,
Now you pay for someone with no love to give,
Too late you ask for a return I cannot give,
I Salamander smile as you cry and I watch you burn,
And through the flames I move on.

This really needed to come out, it was inspired by "Hey Jupiter" by Tori Amos and her words and video that still make me cry silent tears and give me adrenaline flows, they take me right back to my decision to "Wait and see".

Melysza Jackson
I Stand Alone

Darkness cloaks many desires,
Broken
Beaten
Hidden within
Fear of falling, in the land of trust
My heart, my soul has seen this pain
Light has fooled me twice before
Fantasies won't appear anymore
Choking
Drowning
Anxieties win
Tears feed my demon who lies within
I walk the sands always alone
Searching for light to carry me home

Broken

Beaten down and broken
Knotted pile of thread, such disaster to unravel
comes a price of her two sides
Silent pain, from the voices of the wicked
Fallen tears, as the blade deepens into her flesh

The angelic voice sings his melody, as he draws her soul to his command

The endless screams from the voices that plague her thoughts, silencing themselves for one sweet moment… in fear
'come here child'
Death whispers, extending his hand to her
'you are home'
Death sneers under his cloak

A shallow breath rises from her chest
Her body thrashes against Death's song
As her soul cries for another angel
But does he not hear her plea

For now, the reaper's grip tightens his hold on the knotted threads of her soul
Wrapping it tightly against her throat, silencing her cries for another angel

Silent pain,   Fallen tears
Another death song sings

19 and Foolish

A reckless dreamer, lives in her clouds of safety
Whispered truths with lies woven throughout
She lays on the dewy grass, disconnecting from the now
Brought down from the haven of her protective cloud

A single tear trembles, unsure of how to release the foolish girl's fear
The helpless night has brought upon a chill of anger, the hoot of the owl no longer exists
Not a single cloud remains
Abandoned
Alone

The stars weep as the once wild dreamer, now leaves her dreams behind
Ripped across the razored grass, by the monster who now holds her down, with eyes full of perverted lust
As the foolish dreamer cringes with hatred and disgust

With vacant eyes she stares above, lost in a hell now called home
Aimlessly the foolish girl wanders, with no clouds to take her home

Razors Edge

Razors edge glides upon her ivory flesh
Grasping hold of some kind of semblance (guise)
Hearing hated words otherwise
Begging to feel, until the razor peels back her hidden heart and tormented thoughts
She holds the blade against her flesh, watching red tears flow
Drip by drip she loses grip of her inner lights glow
Guilt kicks in, with her hidden sin, but wicked names still hurt her
Broken bones always heal, but beaten names seal the deal
As the razors edge takes its final meal, forever more

Starving Heart

Mirror Mirror on the wall
She is the ugliest of them all
Starved by love and food embrace
She slides her meals from her face
Fading from her beautiful soul
Her thoughts have become dark as coal
Volatile
Lost
Thin and weak
She has starved now for a week
Ribs and bones she now wears

The Queen's vindictive words have caught her in a gnarly snare
Jealous fingers upon her neck
Moss green eyes scream within, as she grows so very thin
Mirror Mirror on the wall she was beautiful after all, only she knew it before her fall

Darkness Depressed

Fat I am now fated
Slut you have now stated
Stupid is constant and hated
Grim reaper stands there elated
For the broken and berated
Grim holds me here in his darkened realm
Whispers come from my turbulent hell
I reach for light that never exists
Sins fill my head with a self-inflicted list
Where can I find my one true wish
Tears fall to break free from their chains
Beaten by my mind's hard cane
Pressed and Depressed
Save me, or put me to rest

R A Bane
Opium Dreams

Midnight screams and opium dreams
Things cannot be as they seem
This figure that stands before me now
A vision from my past somehow
Long has my love been in the ground
And my heart has made a mournful
sound
Must be a vision born of this smoke
On which even now I do choke
The vapors usually subdue the pain
But these play havoc on my heart and brain
The wind gently dances through her hair
As her body seemly floats through the air
How can such a lovely vision
Bring the torturing solace of a prison
Now she does to me draw nearer
With every step, my heart grows dearer
Please Lord stops this madness
When the smoke clears nothing but sadness
But before me she does now stand
Reaching out to take my hand
It is solid not vapor or cold
But warm flesh that I hold
Sanity now escaping me
Mind and body fill with ecstasy
We danced away the night

Ending all worries and strife
It seemed like we were dancing on air
When I looked down to see my body lying there
A tear of joy ran down my face
For I knew she came to take me to my rightful place
Forever by her side
Not just a vision in my mind
So let my flesh fall from the bone
I am forever home

Farewell

Walk with me to a place I know too well

Walk with me to the very gates of hell
Let me have just one last embrace
And of your lips one final taste
Before I make my way into the dark
You shall always be within my heart
For your soul is too pure for where I must tread
Much too beautiful for all the fear and dread
But for my sins I must atone
And make this journey on my own
So here you will stay
When I turn to make my way
They say that true love never dies
In that way, we will always be alive
I feel the warmth of your flesh in that last kiss
As I turn to walk into that dark abyss
They say that demons do not cry
Tell that to the tear falling from my eye

Elaine Bezuidenhout
Blood Red Rose

A blood red rose he shared,
My finger it then pricked,
And yet I held on still,
I smelled the sweetest scent,
It to my breast I pressed,
By its thorns my heart pierced,
My love song I sang still,
Blinded by its sweet smell,
Through the scar my face paled,
But still closer I pressed,
Deeper the thorns went still,
Now that rose has blackened,
Of crimson price it claimed,
Yet I pressed it closer still.

Eleventh Hour

She sat on a rock of hope through all her time,
But it started to crumble, erode this hour,
Light turned to dusk, dusk turned to a dark hour,
But still she held on to this little heap of powder,
Maybe, just maybe there is still time,
Maybe he will still come,
Then the winds started to blow,
Little by little the sand moved beneath her,
Will he still come in this the eleventh hour?
The last of the sand started to move now,
She started to fall, though she tried to hold on,
But it was the end of her last hour,
Eleventh, the eleventh hour was too long,
So long she waited, but he did not come,
Her hope faded, she could no longer hold on,
He was too late, he took too long,
Eleventh, the eleventh hour was too long.

The Soul That Could Not Find Love

With everyone she loved,
Still present in her heart,
The heart now grows cold,
The soul gets weary,
Her thoughts turn dreary,
All her hope fades away,
Death her biggest wish,

She sits alone at night,
And by herself she sighs,
Thinking of ones she loved,
Lovers she gave her heart,
Who tore her heart apart,
She still feels the pain,

And in the early hours,
When she at last slumbers in,
The nightmares still come,
When the sun warms her face,
She does not want to wake.

James D. Merwin
The Ferryman's Journey

I am in the midst of my madness
Inside, a beast in me swells
The ferryman invites me into his boat
And I hear the toll of the bells

Across the river Styx, is where we now go
And along the turbulent waves
I see the departed that once took my ride
And slowly the beast in me raves

Mumbling sounds that are incoherent to some
But to me the sounds ring of truth
I understand what the beast is now saying
I have understood my possessor since youth

I have lived with it in times of sadness
I have lived with it in times of joy
No one has ever seen my tormentor
For he is invisible and also so coy

He does not want the world to see him
He uses me as a shield from the world
I keep him inside in seclusion
And for this, into battle, I'm hurled

I walk in a path of delusion
For he tells me when I'm lost, he will find

The way that we so need to travel
And in my sickness I listen, for I am not in my right mind

I look up at the "Ferryman" to thank him
"Why thank me", he says, so sincere
"The river Styx is the river to hell"
"Why are you not filled with fear"

With tears in my eyes, I explain
And I tell him I did not cross alone
You have saved me in a way you can't fathom
For the beast in me now has come home

"It is a price I was willing to pay"
"For the beast to finally be free"
"I want him to feel the pain"
"That through my life, he has given to me"

I Wonder

Darkness, inexplicably comprehendible
Months upon months pass by
Suddenly, with no permission
I am headed to war
My first moments in this war
Were ones of confusion and pain
People muddled around me with masks
I was torn from the safety of my liquid surroundings
I now must struggle for some answers
Why, if you loved me
Did you push me from the safety of your womb
Did even you, at such a tender age
Know that inside of you
Spawned something destined for nightmares
Is that why I am forced to walk now
Among the evil of this world
Trying just to carve my own niche
A place where I could fit
To find something that could guide me
To hold something that I could cherish
To feel something that is not explainable
To keep something that only I hold dear and close
I abhor your decision to have me live
I now must find a new resting place
I am headed for war
Suddenly, with no permission
Months upon months pass by
Darkness, inexplicably comprehendible
Now encases me in its cold, icy, and eternal arms
It consumes me, at last in my darkness, I am FREE

When Will It

I smile at the torment
I relinquish the fight
I glow in the darkness
I need not the light

In the light is the ugly
In the light is the truth
In the darkness, no nothing
In the darkness, my youth

I feed off the tricks
That play in my head
I listen to voices
And entertain what they said

I jump down the hole
That the rabbit has made
I beg for the exit
From this twisted parade

My thoughts, they march freely
To an insane band leader
Between sanity and hysteria
My life, it now teeters

Just one little push
Is all that I need
To fulfill the dementia

And allow it to lead

It will lead me as always
It will make me think I am well
As it dances the dance
And lead me straight to hell

Paul B. Morris
Hey Maggie

Hey Maggie, I want to keep your smile,
Preserve it for prosperity so I can gaze at your beauty once in a while.
Sorry that the cuts hurt so much and that my hands are unsteady,
I've tried before on others, so I knew that I'd be ready.

Hey Maggie, please do not resist,
It only makes it harder to operate, so please sit still, I really must insist.
I hope you do approve of what I've achieved with your face,
Much harder than anticipated, yet I don't feel that it's a disgrace.

Hey Maggie, I bet this wasn't what you expected?
Neither I, but I felt so much anger when I was cruelly rejected.
Never mind, I'll do my best to correct all of these glitches,
So sorry to say that will mean even more stitches.

Hey Maggie, do not get giving in,
I've planned so much fun for you, working with your skin,
Told you didn't I, that I'd get right within your head,

I couldn't have you when you were alive, but I can keep you now you're dead.

The Grey Man

What mind is this?
One that lives through torture and sufferance.
Thoughts prevail that are not of my own, they are the property of a monster most foul,
Frequently they betray me, these images that dance to the delight of The Grey Man,
It is he who orchestrates my suffering, taking pleasure at the scenes of anguish played out before him.
It is constant.

Day gives in to night, I should be rested in mind,
It fights the need for sleep, afraid of what is to come.
In reality, I have kissed her goodnight as she lies sleeping peacefully,
Yet I witness her demise as she is brutally slain before me, her blood mercilessly drained from her body.
Hopelessly I watch the butchery, restrained and unable to save my love, tears run freely at her passing.
Once more, The Grey Man laughs.

My mind falls easily, ravished by the eyeless beast,
Spreading murder with ease for his pleasure only.
With repeated frequency, time of sleep is punctured,
Innocent blood spilt in the most abhorrent of ways,
offering no respite from the torturous imagery.

Ridiculed yet again by The Grey Man, his laughter grating at my skin,
Until light of day breaks and my soul can take no more.

Lemmy Rushmore
Vestiges

I must sit here and ask
After what came and fled
Am I really alive
Or am I truly dead

I know I'm not myself
At least not what I was
But then who knows these things
Maybe that's what love does

Maybe it comes to take
And not add like it could
Maybe it doesn't give
Like we wish that it would

Maybe it's just a beast
That comes looking to feast
One that picks at our bones
Till the time we're released

Are we only its toys
Are we merely its pets
Does it pick us apart
Without any regrets

It is this I must ask
As I sit in this state
Is the damage to great
Am I really too late

Is there something more left
Than these vestiges seen
Is there something else here
Somewhere hidden between…

This Hell That I'm In

Why have you sent me here
Why have you lent me this
When I've done nothing more
Than to offer you bliss

Why must I face these days
That I'm facing right now
Won't you please let me know
Have I wronged you somehow

Just what was it I did
To deserve all this ache
To have earned all this hurt
What mistake did I make

What on Earth made you choose
To make me suffer so
Why must anguish be mine
I would sure love to know

Was it something I said
Or just some part of me
I just can't understand
What might bring this to be

I tried only to love
And to cherish and care
But you repaid those things
With this world of despair

Remnants

Seems you took a piece here
And you took a piece there
But I didn't much care
I had plenty to share

Just a morsel you'd snatch
Then a smidgen you'd take
But soon hunks you'd hack off
Till I started to ache

Far too trusting I was
Far too naïve it seems
Just a fool and no more
Still believing in dreams

I thought you were the one
So I followed my heart
And I stayed in that place
While you carved me apart

Like a statue I stood
Whilst you chiseled away
With the thought in my head
That there might come a day

But it never came 'round
Not that day I looked for
So just remnants I am
Only that and no more…

Becky Narron
Without You

I can't breathe without you
I can't feel my heart
I don't want to live
If we are apart

My soul is bleeding
My will has come undone
I don't want to go on
How do I carry on?

I can't tell you I love you
You won't understand
I need you beside me
Please tell me you can

Don't let me walk from you
Please fight through the pain
I can't be without you
I have nothing to gain

I'm begging you please
Just hold on real tight
I need you to love me
With all of your might

Linz Bassett
Shattered Trust

Broken bridges cover a cobbled river of shattered stones
Rippling through the mosaic cracks wrapped around my heart
Upon which years of trust precariously teetered
As once again I cower at the infliction of renunciation
Betrayal so blasé and nonchalant my spirit vociferate in rage
Where once there was respect and love but a mere remembrance
Now there is only regret as I combat the birthing of hate
Emotions rendered vacuous in a receptacle of faithlessness
An abolished Angel, broken by naïveté and sciolism
Trust now aught but a crumbled piece of paper
Loyalty obliterated in one fell swoop
Another lesson learned

New Beginnings

Broken wings mending in a wondrous awakening
As you step away from the stormy callous antagonist
That for so long immersed you in the twilight of tribulation
Close the door on its acrimonious and contemptuous villainy
Face the sunshine that gleams winsomely in
The morning hue that blossoms with the rising sun
Its rays coruscating like a mirage in the distance
The future hungered and coveted for so long now within reach

A destiny scribed in words filled with so much elegance and yearning
Words that bound our hearts together long before we met
Words that reached out over the ebb of distance
And thread its way through our souls
Enticing us to continue on this wondrous path
Shepherding us to consummation

Believe and trust in the magic of new beginnings
And embrace our destiny as fate has proclaimed
Warmth suffuses the chambers of your heart
Restoring the battered anguish that tortured your soul
In the blackness of persecution for so long
Break thee free, envelop the love that unconditionally
Offers absolution above all and beyond
 A love that is yours to keep

I Am Empty

The emptiness hounds the darkness of the night
As my lost soul seeks and does not find.
I watch blackness turn to gray
Until the golden glow of dawn shimmers.
Sleep is no more, as I wait
For one word, one smile
The salvation for my concern
To dissolve the shadows that settled
With the silence, you left behind.
My heart beats but I do not comprehend
For my heart lies there within you
Encapsulating you soul
Until you find you way.

Let the Past Go

A dewy mist clouds your eyes
As memories resound in your mind
Oh my, love, no more.

Now is the time
To let the past unwind
Purge your soul, my love
Leave the hurt behind

For you have so much love to give
And so much passion to share
Let it be
Find your happiness with me

Come, let us wash it all away
My love so pure and free
Is yours forevermore

The Dark Side of Love

Everyone has a dark side
A deep dark place to hide their demons
Fearing its escape in a darkest moment
I have seen some of yours
I know you're not perfect
I know you've felt pain and hurt
I know you've been betrayed

And even though you think it might
And you try to push me away
Know this my love
It's your demons that drives me wild
It's those secrets, the pain and despair
That makes me love you even more

And all the darkness in the world
Cannot extinguish the light inside me
For my love is your light
Come into the light, my love
I am waiting

Gerri R. Gray
Today I Feel

Today I feel like shards of glass,
Mirrored pieces disarranged,
Like Sylvia Plath, her head in the oven,
      Never speaking to God again.

Gone are my treasures, bright and shining,
Vacant now my chest of hopes.
Pierced with silence, noblest of hearts,
      No parting consolation gifts.

Today I feel like mist and shadow,
Disconnected, etherized,
A swirling mirage, a stranger impassive,
Like Lady Macbeth to madness driven.

Today I feel like staring at fire
Until my eyes are burned of tears.
Today I feel like dancing on graves
  Until the earth opens
    And swallows my pain.

Dark Craving

From my grave of wilted roses
  when the moon is waning and pale,
shall I awaken and arise,
  cloaked in midnight's veil.

To ride the wind and taste the night,
  inhale deeply the scent of the living,
And bask in death's exquisite delight,
  so cruel,
  so perfect,
  so unforgiving.

My heart beats not, but still it longs;
  my eyes weep not, but grieve in sorrow.
Shrouded dreams haunt like a ghost;
  I thirst with each tomorrow.

Upon your warmth, I will hungrily feast
  and drink my fill of scarlet mirth,
'Til dreamless slumber calls with dread
  and earth once more becomes my bed.

When darkness veils the bleeding sun
  and light of day becomes forsaken,
When my flesh the shadows caress,
  again shall I awaken.

What a wicked thing forlorn,

a morbid riddle have I become.
Suffering is my nourishment;
 for me, peace is there none.

Weep not for me
 but for thyself,
 and pray for thine own soul to save.
For all that you fear and loathe of me
 is what your secret self does crave.

Memento Mori (Christmas Eve)

I gazed into the silver mirrored balls
That hung from boughs of plastic evergreen.
I pondered the reflection that they showed;
A face that looked familiar, yet so strange.
The colored lights danced in the stranger's eyes
With red, green, yellow, and the saddest blue.
The melancholy Christmas memories
Brought emptiness within and tears without.
I saw within the shiny orbs of glass
A child as bleak as gray December snow.
Her frozen eyes of desolation wept,
Her fragile hand reached ghost-like out for mine.
Then one by one the ornaments did fall
And shatter into shards upon the floor.
Distorted, broken, lifeless like my soul
And sharp enough to slice through pulsing veins.
A silent scream was heard inside my head,
The first cut is the deepest one of all.
A crimson ocean danced inside my dreams
And washed away all traces of her pain.

Richard Archer
Cursed

When the moon covers his eyes,
the scorned woman with fire on her brow
and hardness in her heart,
approaches the sacred tree.
A white dress hides her black purpose.

Placing a nail with trembling reverence
she drives it into the wood.
Then nail after nail is hammered in
accompanied by her
whispered curse.

Her ex-lover sleeps fitfully,
sweat on his forehead he snaps awake.
Pinned he twists and turns
puncture wounds spreading and
staining.

When he is found he is pale white,
a bloodless spirit,
a contorted shell.
His lifeless face imitating
a Noh mask.

In her garden, the revenged woman
Buries her hammer and sap

coated nails in a polished
wooden box.
Burying her memories.

For what is left of the night
She sleeps.
The white dress crackles
on the hearth.
Warming her smiling face.

Book Lover

I loved her but she loved books,
For me she never spared a look.
As she only loved the printed page,
It was to books her heart she gave.

Her cook book showed how to crack eggs,
So I cracked it over her head.
Splintering her skull into tiny parts
Fracturing it, like she broke my heart.

As she whimpered I turned to her skin,
Flaying it nice and thin.
Then with blood drawn from her faltering heart,
On her wet flesh I made red art.

While she took her last breath,
I made a book cover from her dress.
Then stapled in her pages of damp flesh,
But I wasn't finished yet.

I put her eyes on the front page,
Strengthening it with pieces of rib cage.
Then after smearing it all with her brain,
I read her story over and over again.

What happened to the book after I don't know?
It bored me, so I just let it go.
My love for her had simply stopped,

So I think I left it in an unsuspecting book shop.

Perhaps you'll find it staining a shelf
Its bloody secrets eager to get out.
If you think you've found my book,
Will you be brave enough to chance a look?

Mathias Jansson
Confessions of Adrian Black - ghosts that I have fucked

Countess Marybeth

In the north of Scotland in an old castle
Haunted by strange ghost and ghouls
I spent a night between red satin sheets
Laying back in the bed looking at the fire place
When she rose from the ashes

Burning hot with flames licking her corpse
The young countess Marybeth
An angel with black fingernails
The cunt of burning desire

Paralyzed I laid stiff in my bed
When her nudeness approached
I was aroused by shame and terribly afraid
When her long black nails scratch my legs
And with a serpent's tongue licked my balls
I could feel her breath of death so near

When I entered her burning cave
I felt the sensation of hell's flames eating me inside
All night I was burning with pleasure
But when she left in the morning
My candle had burnt out
And all that was left was ashes of my fire

Lady Morgana

Lady Morgana drowned in a bathtub
Before her wedding day
Stands dripping wet over my head
I taste her salty fountain
Licking every drop from her virgin lips
Driving me insane with thirst
Digging deeper with my tongue
Into the spring of ecstasy
To extinguish my unbearable thirst
Until I hear her screams of pleasure
And she sinks down on my head
Through the bed and vanish as a ghost
Leaving me alone, mad and insane
With my burning fever of fire

The Borgia's twin

So sweet eighteen
The opposite attractions
Dark and blonde
Wild and timid
Caught in their sinful actions
Condemned by the convent
Bricked alive in the wall
Hundreds of years waiting
Now in front of me on the floor
Yearning, crawling so horny
Eager to drag me to the altar
And let me taste their pink oblates
Drink the sweet wine from their cups of sins
Together we will preach the threesome of divinity
Speaking in tongues of cunninglingus
Until they nail me to the cross to teach me
The passion of painful fucking
In every possible position on hard wood

Madame Marie

The corridors of the old brothel
Echoes empty under my step
Suddenly a trembling
A sound of thunder
And from the floor down under
Six muscular men in doggy style
Pulling the golden cart
Of hell's fat whore
In full shining armor
Madame Marie naked
In black high heel boots

She pulls over
And rolls over my body
Like a howling storm
An ocean of breast, stomach, and thighs
As waves on a foaming beach
She rides my hard rocks

I struggle to get some air
Before I sink into the depth
Of her sweaty flesh
I feel the horror of suffocation
The heaven and hell
Of autoerotic asphyxiation

Schoolmistress Susan

Nails on a black board
I feel the chills deep in my bones
I see her shadow
A thin dress of red satin
Transparent with moon light
Revealing every pleasure behind
When she opens the curtains
To her steamy meat scene

Schoolmistress Susanne standing by my side
Still with the rope dangling from her neck
Her skull face burning with red lipstick
The strict mistress of yearning
Eager to learn and punish me

Naked I have to stand
In the naughty corner
Where she teaches me to
Sharpen my pencil
Against her hard, shiny ass
And not to spill my ink
On her white sheet of lace
After a long night
Tired after performing French verbs
She finally let me taste her warm cookie
And whispered satisfied
In my ear that I was a good boy

Glen Damien Campbell
Virginia

They're burning again
The smell of sweat thickens the air
Virginia's thoughts conspire in whispers
"Do you feel it, bitch?
Behold this heavenly incest."
Or is that the Devil in her ear?
She wonders if they will notice her
Standing there, watching them
Muffled in black night
Suffocated by darkness
Alone in parasitic fear
The woman begs, "Kiss me again before I die!"
And he kisses her violently
Virginia presses her hands to her eyes
Quite suddenly she feels misshapen now
Hands sticky with coagulating blood
Breath taken by a thought;
What she is seeing is for her eyes
And her eyes only

John T. M. Herres
Silent Screams

Life behind these padded walls, as surreal as a dream
   A dream where even silence screams, but only silent screams
      Silent screams of ancient Queens beheaded on a stage
The stage, surrounded by noisy throng
   Some hawking wares secured with tongs
      Some yammering of someone else's wrongs
One standing above, above any reproach
   Heralding merits and valiant deeds like a coach
      A coach who stores the team behind padded walls
Yes, life behind these padded walls, wishing t'were a dream
   For here, unlike in dreams, the silence screams, but not silent screams
      Not silent screams from ancient Queens beheaded on a stage.

Gocni Schindler
Bi-Polar Super Bitch

This tale ain't no goddamn good
Was from a time
Chasing that fictional butterfly
Love, within a pretty-little-pink
She fooled me with a good act!
Easy pickings
Just another chump to run through the mud
First date, heaven on earth
Should have seen the wedding bells.
Sweetest little thing
She had the looks
Knew how to manipulate
Fool I be the fool I am!
A bad cartoon character!
With a defective dowsing rod
I'm following her around
It's all honey and biscuits for a week or two
These eyes, filled with lusting hearts
Skulls really, pretending to be love
Floating through the sky
Coonhound salivating at the mouth
'Come back little hearts, come back!'
I'm given the middle finger
Followed by some fish lips
Sour grapes in the bathroom
Then I'm introduced to girlfriend number two
Enter the demon of doom
Raving Psychotic

Calling me a cheater
Ingenuine
Bastard son of a bitch degenerate
Monkey fucker with a small pickle
How did she know?
Paying her bills
Getting her kids to bed
Making lunches
She's out at the bar
Getting wasted
Whore playing at Two AM!
Coming home six steps past the grave
She's with her boyfriend
His name is Rage
Cussing me up and down
Throwing shit around
Tension, so thick, if it was food
Would feed an army for a month
Going out with other guys
She called them 'Good-Ol'boys!'
If only she got paid
Her five kids
Scattered across the room
Call this place a morgue
Didn't give a shit
Bitch is on a five-day bender
Haze of white dust upon the counter
Needles line the floor
Kids crying for food
Fridge is empty
Filling the recycling bin
Six hundred and change in empty liquor
She resembles a walking corpse

Sleep screaming at me for more money
There went rent again!
Back at the tavern, she's hard at it!
I'm putting her kids to bed
Lost to her disorder
I'd call this professionalism
I'm refusing to talk
She out back drinking a bottle of Jack or was it Scotch?
My confusion fills my illusion
Some guy bought it for her she states!
Sucked him off in-between her laughs and swigs
Time for me to fly
Super bitch was on the phone
Waste spouts out of her sewage hole
"I'm callin the cops, mother-fucker!"
"You're going to jail, going to get you outta here!"
She dials Nine-One-One
Packing my shit, time to hit the road like quick
Cops are at the door
In they come
Asking me the ins
Drilling me for the outs
'Officer, I'm just packing my stuff and then I'm gone!'
Shitting my drawers
Convicted Felon
They just want a chance
Place me on the cross again
I contest
'I didn't touch her!'
I'm suddenly viewing my life in past tense
The other officer is talking with her

Two officers having a pow-wow
My bags are almost packed
They approach me
Asking me
'Is she always like this?'
I just nod my head for 'yes'!
Officer
"I'll help you pack"
Shit is in the car
I'm down the road
Not rearview gazing
An hour later
Text message: Come Back
Living a horrific Lifetime experience
My only response
Fuck that!
She tried getting me for rent
I told her to get bent
She hooked up with another drunk
Haven't heard from her since
Never want to see that version of psycho again
Love is that butterfly
Titled the insect of fiction
Simply a working of nonsense
That I tend to get involved with

Leah Negron
Inner Demons

You said you loved
No one else above me
I caught you with her
Ripping my heart in two
I lost my mind in a terrible rage
I killed you both and
Buried you in a single grave
Now here I am
My inner demons constantly
Clawing at me day and night.
 Depression, despair,
Suicidal thoughts.
Fighting with all my might
To not let them win this fight.
Looking for the slightest ray of light
To grasp so that I may banish
Them back to hell before
My soul is lost.
Becoming a Demon myself
With no more light.

Too Tight

He held on too tight
With all of his might
Giving her a fright
Until late one night
He snuffed out her light
Burning her, standing in the firelight
He watched on in delight
As the hours passed bringing on daylight
Now he thought of his plight
He had his first fright
Someone would look for her
That was his oversight
Time for him to pack up
And take flight
Before the passing of
Another night

Death's Poet

I am a poet for the dead
I keep your skull as a reminder
Of what happens
To those who betray me
When I need inspiration
I hold you in my hands and
Remember how I killed you and
Cleaned your flesh from your bones
You thought to use and abuse me
Now you're my play toy
And I use you!

Craig Detheridge
Chocolate Box Love

So happy holding hands
And walking in the park
Stealing sweetest kisses
Lips luscious in the dark
Stupid Cupid's arrow
That falls from up above
Soon melts in the hot sun
That's Chocolate Box Love

All the sugar sweet mice
Run in the pouring rain
Left with just the tails of string
And tales of hurt and pain
Sweet soon turns to poison
Poisons the turtle dove
Lost love leaves only hatred
That's Chocolate Box Love

The Old Fallow Field - *A Rhyming Horror Story*

The land could tell tales, with these fallow pastures, and most of the stories would be considered disasters.

We know of the ones from the war, you see. Also, the hangings from the old oak tree.

Some tell of hobos who camped on the edges, and how something had beat them, no mercy, with sledges.

One told a tale of a little boy, who had just gotten his wish for his favorite toy. He went to play in the field his Daddy just plowed, and later could be heard screaming real loud.

His parents had looked, as did everyone; none found a clue- not even one.

This event is not isolated. Not at all, by far. Did I tell the one of the speeding car?

It came 'round the corner; careening, it seems. A mile away, one could hear tire screams. The car broke through the rail meant to stop them, and flew through the air- The people were locked in. It spun in mid-flight, the car hit the ground, the top ripped off as it tumbled around. If anyone saw it, telling loses its meaning, describing the sound of metal squealing and screaming.

The scene flipped stomachs of those arrived first.

But that isn't even the tale that is worst.

A long time ago, in stories it goes; A farmer tried to get roots from the mounds as they froze. The rain posed a problem of another kind, and made the dirt in the valleys act like unrelenting slime.

He slipped and fell, and broke his left leg; right as his horse ran off with the sled. The man tried to crawl to the house far away; his wife would save him and keep Death at bay!

Before he made it, even half way, he drowned in the mud in that field that day.

Through all of the stories, one thing is uncertain: One important fact, hidden behind a curtain. None can relate the strangeness thus; when most first hear of it, the first word is a cuss.

Oh! Did I tell you of the party thrown by teens? That night there were horrid, blood-curdling screams!

In the trees hid a convict, recently escaped. The dark of the night kept his presence draped. Only too late the kids learned he hid there, as he attacked before any had become aware.

A Priest got called, people thought it a Demon. He went in with his tools, 'He's safe,' they were thinking.

He could be heard reciting certain rituals. The incense smoke rising in soft, gentle curls. The smoke began swirling with violent motion. The weeds swaying from such a virulent commotion. He could be heard, still, hollering over the noise, his cross held up high, perfectly poised.

The people standing on the edges of the scene, could not say what happened; none had seen.

Speculation revolves around the cursed location, on why there exist such heinous creations. Most deal with religion, or lack thereof, saying "The Devil slipped in, like a hand in a glove."

The ones who don't heed all of the warnings, are the ones who end up as new story adornings. For any who've ventured into that field, have gone missing regardless of weapons they wield. A pistol or rifle, knife, or sharp stick, all rendered useless against dark forces so thick.

Whatever the cause of the patch of bad land, something dark, in the making, must have offered a hand.

Now that you've heard the history; I'll tell you what this has to do with me:

My Sister had come over, late one night. We ended up having a terrible fight. She left while still mad, and slammed the door. Rattled the shelves, stuff fell on the floor. I felt some rage that she didn't feel the same as I when bad things I revealed.

Her route took her by the Old Fallow Field; when that hit me, I hoped fate had not sealed her time as she went by that dreadful place, for I wanted that not to be the last I saw her face.

I jumped in my car, sped in pursuit; too bad I had no one else to recruit. I hurriedly chased her to keep her away from the Fields destined to take both of us that day. I neared the curve in the highway going way too fast. Like many before, I died in the crash.

Now for the thing I mentioned before; the thing that is stranger than all of the gore. Not one single body has been recovered, not even the farmer who the mud smothered.

So, I tell you outright, stay away, don't go in! It just may spell your doom, your…

END

Shanta Nicole
Be Still, My Love

Be still my love, rest your weary head
Should I sing you a lullaby or remain quiet instead?
I can hear your heart race, feel your breath at my feet
Not much longer now love, soon I'll be free

I continue my movements, dig into the ground
The pounding of your heart, the only sound
Your hands are tied, your mouth is bound
Memories of our love go round and round

I poke at your flesh, watch you bleed through the sheet
Be quiet my love, for soon you will sleep

Xtina Marie
He Doesn't Know

I lurk in the shadows
watching every move he makes
he pretends not to notice
he's every breath that I take

In my room I paste his pictures
over every inch of my wall
randomly I block my number
and his cell phone, I then call

He greets me rather warmly
and I tingle from the sound
his voice swims through my head
and I sink down to the ground

With my knife, I graze my skin
and carve his name into my wrist
the blood starts to bead now
and I clench my hand into a fist

His voice carries through the phone
as he asks me who this is
and I imagine those lips upon me
as we share our first kiss

The line goes dead and my rage grows fast
I hope he knows just what he's done
with my arm still bleeding, I race from my room
to prove to him I am the one

I sneak through his house so quietly
touching his belongings as I creep

make my way carefully to his room
so I can watch him as he sleeps

I move in closer to his bed
and trace my fingers down his form
I feel his breath upon my face
his exhales rather warm

A drop of blood from my wrists
splatters his white sheet red
but he does not know my arm is not
the only thing that has bled

I kiss the air beside his face
and back out of his room
my rage starts to ebb away
knowing I'll see him very soon

Love Isn't Enough (A Microshort)

"It's over," she said, grabbing her sweater and slipping it over her thin shoulders. It was spring, but there was still a snap to the air, especially in the early morning hours. "What's over?" He looked towards her, his coffee halfway to his lips. "Us," she said, making her way to the door. "Don't you love me anymore?" he asked, no emotion in his voice. "I'll always love you," she met his gaze as the door creaked opened. "But sometimes, love isn't enough."

Love Kills

It's not you, it's me
he whispers in the night
and she knows for certain
that she will never be all right

Her eyes well with tears
when he walks out that door
and she clutches her chest
as she sinks quietly to the floor

Her mouth opens in a scream
but no sound emerges
she wishes for the pain
because she knows that it purges

But she's numb, so numb
because without him she is nothing
she tears at her hair
hoping to feel something

Hot tears make their way
slowly down her cheeks
and she tries to pull herself up
but her legs are too weak

She crawls across the floor
sobbing her silent cries
and she wishes he'd remembered
that she was okay with the lies

What you didn't know
well, she's sure it couldn't hurt
but this? this pain is death
and he's looking forward to the flirt

Her hand closes around the knife
it's cool to the touch
and she's happy to feel anything
because for a while there, there wasn't much

Will it hurt, to plunge it deep?
no worse than the pain she's in now
she plays it over her skin
sweat building on her brow

The knife clatters to the floor
and she lays still
feeling her life slip away
thinking that love kills

a most horrible pain

i cower in the corner, scared of every start, i wish you'd just hit me, instead of tearing out my heart...

i could live with a bruise, or even a black eye, but what you took from me, will cause me to die...

i grab my chest in pain, why does this hurt so much? if i had known this, i would have said no to your touch...

from the minute we met, you started to poison my veins, i can feel it throughout, a most horrible pain...

i curl up in fear, and my heart screams "why?!" but death does not come, so i lay prone and cry...

i'm still lying here, on the floor in a ball, there is nothing left, you've taken it all...

you raise your foot again, just another kick, when i stopped being "love", and turned into "chick"...

you step over me as you go, you don't even seem to care, i reach out as you pass, but i'm only touching air...

i try to cry out, and beg for my life, you look back, to hand me the knife...

i'm too weak to grasp it, i ask you to plunge deep,
and you oblige me, my heart- yours to keep...

you continue to leave, and make your way to the
door, i slowly bleed out, yours forever more...

Her Love Has No End

She caresses his face
ever so softly
tells him she loves him
so very fondly

She kisses his lips
runs her fingers through his hair
breathes him in deeply
as if he were her air

She tells him "I love you,"
again and again
wanting him to know
her love has no end

She whispers in his ear
she will only ever be true
tells him that it was her heart
in which that he drew

She cuddles him to her chest
so that he can sleep
waits 'til his breathing
becomes rather deep

She runs her fingers over his body
a smile on her lips
disentangles herself slowly
as from his arms she slips

Long and hard she stares at his face

every inch
brushes aside the misgivings
the doubt just a twinge

In her heart she knows
that this is what she must do
and she wonders deep down
if he has a clue

She knows that she'll miss him
he was her one true love
She slits his throat in his sleep
and feels the warmth of his blood

She lays with his corpse, the clock by the bed
ticking away the time
and she whispers in the quiet
"Now he will forever be mine."

HellBound Books

Other poetry titles from HellBound Books for your delectation…

DARK MUSINGS

Available at www.hellboundbookspublishing.com

Dark Musings by Xtina Marie

The perfect companion piece to Light Musings – The dark side of Xtina Marie's poetry delves into intense emotions: heartache, loss, hurt, pain, rage, and a dangerous consuming love which can drive one insane. Dark Musings is not a collection!

The author returned to the centuries old practice of Narrative Poetry—the telling of a story through poetry. If you believe you are brave enough to explore the savage emotions of the human heart; Dark Musings will test your mettle.

LIGHT MUSINGS

Available at www.hellboundbookspublishing.com

Light Musings by Xtina Marie

The perfect companion piece to Dark Musings – an intriguing mirror image of the darkness you have just read, but no less deep and soul stirring.

What a web she weaves. Light Musings is a poetic narrative—a story told through related poems. Xtina Marie is a master of this style. Known by her fans as the Dark Poet Princess, this term of endearment came about as a result of the horror genre embracing her first book: Dark Musings which continues to garner stellar reviews. Light Musings will not disappoint her loyal fans as darkness is present within these pages as well. However, this latest book will show a much larger audience that Xtina's poetry pulls out every feeling the reader has ever experienced—forcing them to feel with her protagonist. Light Musings shows us that love is made from darkness and light; something Xtina Marie explores like no one else.

Other HellBound Books Titles

Worship Me

Something is listening to the prayers of St. Paul's United Church, but it's not the god they asked for; it's something much, much older.

A quiet Sunday service turns into a living hell when this ancient entity descends upon the house of worship and claims the congregation for its own. The terrified churchgoers must now prove their loyalty to their new god by giving it one of their children or in two days time it will return and destroy them all.

As fear rips the congregation apart, it becomes clear that if they're to survive this untold horror, the faithful must become the faithless and enter into a battle against God itself. But as time runs out, they discover that true monsters come not from heaven or hell… …they come from within.

No Rest For The Wicked

A modern day ghost story with its skeletons buried firmly in the past.

From beyond the grave, a murderous wife seeks to complete her revenge on those who betrayed her in life; a powerless domestic still fears for her immortal soul while trying to scare off anyone who comes too close; and the former plantation master - a sadistic doctor who puts more faith in the teachings of de Sade than the Bible

When Eric and Grace McLaughlin purchase Greenbrier Plantation, their dreams are just as big as those who have tried to tame the place before them. But, the doctor has learned a thing or two over his many years in the afterlife, is putting those new skills to the test, and will go to great lengths in order to gain the upper hand. While Grace digs into the death-filled history of her new home, Eric soon becomes a pawn of the doctor's unsavory desires and rapidly growing power, and is hell-bent on stopping her.

Sángre: The Color of Dying

Carlos Colón's first published novel is the story of Nicky Negrón, a Puerto Rican salesman in New York City who is turned into foul-mouthed, urban vampire with a taste for the undesirables of society such as sexual predators, domestic abusers and drug dealers.

A tragic anti-hero, Nicky is haunted by profound loss. When his life is cut short due to an unforeseen event at the Ritz-Carlton, it results in a public sex scandal for his surviving family. He then rises from the dead to become a night stalker with a genetic resistance that enables him to retain his humanity, still valuing his family whilst also struggling to somehow maintain a sense of normalcy.

Simultaneously described as haunting, hilarious, horrifying and heartbreaking, Sángre: The Color of Dying is a breathtakingly fun read.

HellBound Books

Demons, Devils & Denizens of Hell Volume I

A hellish collection of short stories from some of the best in the business - compiled by the award-winning author P. Mattern.

Featuring tales from the darkest pits of hades by, Tania Hagan, Lily Luchesi, Jay Michael Wright II, Ken Goldman, Sergio "ente per ente" Palumbo, Emery LeeAnn, Crystal Barnard, James H Longmore, Toneye Eyenot, James Richardson, Lori Fontanez, Marcus Mattern, Lance Tuck, L. Ashby, P. Mattern, Elizabeth Cash, Bryan A. Tann, Elizabeth Zemlicka, Michael Sutton, Thomas S. Gunther, Feind Gottes, and the incomparable Nik Kerry

Beautiful Tragedies - A Dark Poetry Anthology

The Big Book of Bootleg Horror

Twenty tales of terror, darkness, the truly macabre and things most unpleasant from a delectably eclectic bunch of the very best independent horror authors on the scene today:

S.E. Rise, Kevin Wetmore, Paul Stansfield, Craig Stwewart, Shaun Avery, Jeff Meyers, Marc DeWit, Timothy Wilkie, Quinn Cunningham, Melanie Waghorne, Marc E. Fitch, Stanley B. Webb, Tim J. Finn, Ken Goldman, Ralph Greco Jr, Roger Leatherwood, Vincent Treewell, David Owain Hughes, J.J. Smith and the inimitable James H. Longmore

In this superlative tome, HellBound Books have embraced the taboo, gone all-out to horrify and have broken the flimsy boundaries of good taste to make The Big Book of Bootleg Horror the perfect anthology for those who take their horror like we take our coffee - insidiously dark and most definitely unsweetened.

HellBound Books

Shopping List

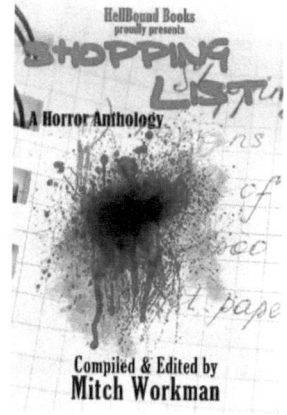

A simply superlative collection of spine-tingling horror from the very best minds in the business!

We decided upon the shopping list theme for this particular volume as an antithesis to those wildly successful writers (they know who they are) of whom it is often said *'we would read their damned shopping list if they published it!'*.

Well, we have given twenty-one of the hottest authors in the independent horror scene the unique opportunity to have their own shopping lists read by you - along with their most terrifying tales of course!

Stories of gut-wrenching terror from:

Kathy Dinisi, Robert Over, Christopher O'Halloran, Eric W. Burgin, Russ Gartz, Mark Slada, Jeff Baker, Tim Miller, Nick Swain, JC Raye, Jovan Jones, Ben Stevens, David F. Gray, Brandon Cracraft, M.S. Swift, Kevin Holton, David Owain Hughes, Bertram Allan Mullin, Jeff C. Stevenson, Sebastian Crow and S.E. Rise

Beautiful Tragedies - A Dark Poetry Anthology

**A HellBound Books LLC
Publication**

www.hellboundbookspublishing.com

Printed in the United States of America

www.ingramcontent.com/pod-product-compliance
Lightning Source LLC
Chambersburg PA
CBHW021122300426
44113CB00006B/256